DISRUPTION

Adweek Books is designed to present interesting, insightful books for the general business reader and for professionals in the worlds of media, marketing, and advertising.

These are innovative, creative books that address the challenges and opportunities of these industries, written by leaders in the business. Some of our writers head their own companies, others have worked their way up to the top of their field in large multinationals. But they share a knowledge of their craft and a desire to enlighten others.

*We hope readers will find these books as helpful and inspiring as Ad-*week, Brandweek, *and* Mediaweek *magazines.*

DISRUPTION

Overturning Conventions
and Shaking Up the Marketplace

Jean-Marie Dru

JOHN WILEY & SONS, INC.

New York   ◆   Chichester   ◆   Brisbane   ◆   Toronto
Singapore   ◆   Weinheim

Translated by Robin Lemberg, Sarah Baldwin, and Jean-Marie Dru.

Library of Congress Cataloging-in-Publication Data
Dru, Jean-Marie.
    Disruption : overturning conventions and shaking up the marketplace /
Jean-Marie Dru
        p.   cm.
    Includes bibliographical references.
    ISBN 0-471-16565-4 (alk. paper)
    1. Advertising—Cross-cultural studies.   2. Advertising agencies.
3. Creative ability in business.   I. Title.
HF6178.D78   1996
659.1—dc20   96-21256
                                                            CIP

Printed in the United States of America

10 9 8 7 6 5 4 3

To Marie-Virginie

PREFACE

DISRUPTION IS AT once a method, a way of thinking, and a state of mind.

It is a manner of questioning the way things are, of breaking with what has been done and seen before, of rejecting the conventional. For those who refuse to sit around, who strive to move forward and beyond, Disruption can be a tool. A tool that offers those who want to give birth to new ideas a chance to do just that. There aren't that many new ideas.

The foundation of Disruption is a three-step reasoning process: Convention, Disruption, and Vision. You start by identifying impediments to clear thinking (conventions), and then you throw them into question with an idea that is radically new (a disruption). All this is done with a sense of where you're going, a more or less intuitively divined direction (the vision). This method, born in an advertising agency, was conceived to help create campaigns that are more effective, more intrusive because they represent a profound break with the status quo.

Very quickly, Disruption proved itself to be bigger than advertising. It turned out to be useful for business in general.

For companies, success lies in questioning and mobility. Companies must create new worlds. They must constantly do, undo, and redo. To accomplish this, they must adopt a mind-set of anticipation. They can no longer surf the wave; instead they must become the wind that creates the wave. They are always in need of a vision that is several steps ahead. As we will see, that is where Disruption comes into play. Disruption enables one to envision fresh, innovative strategies and, as a result, larger shares of the future for brands and for companies themselves.

Disruption is a catalyst of the imagination, a guide that opens numerous paths. A system for those who hate systems. A method that encourages reversing perspectives. A process that gives brands new vitality. An alternative to "more-of-the-same" thinking. In a word, Disruption is an agent of change.

The heart of this book lies in Part II, the Disruption Discipline, which includes three chapters: "Disruption," "Convention," and "Vision."

We live in disruptive times. The outside world forces us constantly to "rethink" our ways of thinking. Nothing is fixed or guaranteed any longer. What we once thought was unalterable has suddenly turned out to be fragile, if not transitory. Disruption is a way of getting ready for change, of always being alert. Of saying no to inertia.

In a blur of movement, that which you can clearly distinguish has a stronger identity than that which is immobile. In this unpredictable world, Disruption embodies movement. It helps anticipate the future. It reminds each of us that life is motion.

Jean-Marie Dru

CONTENTS

DISRUPTION

1

INTRODUCTION
Beyond Advertising Borders

YOU CHECK INTO a hotel in another country. The first thing you do when you get to your room is turn on the television. You zap for a while and inevitably come upon a few commercials. They have a tone, a color, a flavor somehow different from those you know. Something indefinable that makes them unlike those you're used to seeing. The reason is simple. Nothing reflects a country and an age better than its advertising. It is the very expression of the values of the times. It is part of a country's collective unconscious. The creatives who conceive ads draw their inspiration from everyday life, from the attitudes that forge a country's identity. "You can tell the ideals of a nation by its advertisements," said a well-known advertiser at the beginning of this century. Through its advertising, your country is showing.

I have always been interested in the differences in advertising throughout the world. As time passes, I believe more and more that the distinctions are pronounced. From one continent to another and even from one country to the next, our work is different. We don't do things the same way. We work by the dictates of our respective cultures. Yet executives at the big agencies believe that advertising from different parts of the globe is becoming increasingly similar. This is not true. They are misled by their common training, their similar organizations and strategic tools, and their

1

shared work processes, in which everything always leads to the same copywriter–art director collaboration. As a result, they make the error of believing that the advertising profession is the same in New York and Paris, in London and Singapore. Global campaigns mislead them as well. While these give a feeling of sameness, in reality, there are no more than 50 of them.

Ideas are rooted in the concrete. They grow out of the daily lives of the art director and the copywriter. A great idea always comes from one person's mind, someone who, by definition, is local. If you place 10 people in Brussels to conceive a European campaign, you'll get nothing. Brief five creative teams in five European capitals, ask them to build the best local campaign, and then maybe you'll have a chance of seeing a campaign that can export itself. If you're lucky. We must, as Tom Peters advises, reverse the old adage and say: "Think local, act global."

Today, the world has changed. And agencies with it. European agencies owe a lot to their American counterparts and to the United States itself. The reason is simple. The United States dominated the postwar world, both economically and culturally. It took on the task of rebuilding a world shattered by a global war and rescued by American forces. The United States and its corporations succeeded at doing just that. With unmatched enthusiasm, they exported capital and know-how to Europe and the Far East, as well as to the rest of the world. They have led the world in marketing and still do. But today there is a difference. The United States is no longer alone. It now has partners where it once had dependents. Europe and the Far East came of age quite a while ago. This, of course, means change. It implies a torrent of ideas from around the world. And people's need to share them with each other.

This also means that we must move constantly from the local to the global, and back to the local again. To achieve this, we cannot look at things from far away. We must not reduce everything to the lowest common denominator. We must not oversimplify. We must realize that all of us can and should enrich ourselves from the experiences of others. Creativity is not generated in a vacuum. A better future for a brand can be inspired by an initiative taken by someone on the other side of the globe. The more sources of inspiration and creativity there are, the more opportunities for new ideas there will be. And this is true for Americans as much as it is for Europeans and Asians. We should always be students of other countries' advertising. In this ever-changing world, you can never be too curious.

That's why I, a Frenchman, have taken the liberty of writing—in English, for international readers—a book about advertising. And, by extension, a book about marketing and business at large. There's no French arrogance in this whatsoever, just a simple desire to build a bridge between advertising cultures.

United States and France

When you start to compare French and American advertising, you realize that there are many differences. That in fact, under the surface, they vary profoundly. This stems first of all from each culture's relationship with business and, more generally, with money. French and American attitudes are complete opposites. And advertising reflects this. On the European side of the Atlantic, the commercial act remains suspect. People rarely trust a salesperson. This leads to very staged commercials and to indirect, almost oblique arguments. Advertising in France is very theatrical. Not so in the United States. Nobody there is shocked by a hard sell. Americans do not fear deadly competition. They cherish brutal pragmatism. There is a real culture of "salesmanship" in the United States. For Americans, advertising is a selling tool like any other. While less than 10 percent of French commercials feature someone who addresses the camera directly, over 70 percent of American commercials do. In the United States, the brand spokesperson looks you directly in the eye. By contrast, in France, the advertiser sells with modesty and reserve.

These differences result from each country's respective traditions and the contrasting attitudes toward business and profit they engender. In the United States, the advertising act is natural. In France, advertising people always try to justify themselves. They seek to seduce rather than to convince. They believe that the very pleasure derived from a beautiful campaign is capable of inciting people to purchase the product. By contrast, the most creative American copywriter, whose work can be just as seductive as a European's, will say within two minutes of presenting his commercials: "It's going to sell." I don't think I've ever heard a creative person in France or the United Kingdom pronounce the word *sell* in front of me in more than 20 years. It's as if this word were incongruous or anachronistic. European creatives look for ideas, and when they are strategic and shrewd, they sell. Their American counterparts are more direct. They look first for what will sell.

Even the way we look for ideas is different. In France, we search first for the idea and then make sure it works with the product's preestablished strategy. There is movement back and forth in the thinking. In the United States, the process functions differently, by iteration. It starts upstream and moves down. I am always struck, at idea meetings in New York, when I see creatives presenting "lines." They never fail to say that what they've come up with is "almost there," as if they've gotten closer to that unspoken, undefined perfect claim. It seems as though they always begin by looking for a theme, a slogan, a signature, as if the ideal exists somewhere, almost transcendentally. The words *idea* and *ideal* resemble each other very much in English. It's as if, for creatives, the idea is the embodiment of an ideal, something to be used as a model but that in reality doesn't exist.

Americans invented hyperrealism and the French, impressionism. This parallel is a little facile, even simplistic. Nonetheless, it is telling. Americans are attached to the concrete, the pragmatic. Their civilization is materialistic. Only reality interests them. I remember an American marketing director once telling me, "The nonquantifiable might as well be nonexistent." The French, who don't share this attitude, are more attracted by ideas and impressions. Both sides are right. They simply react according to their own culture.

The United States has a tradition of writing before visualizing. This is due to the flexibility and the succinctness of the English language. British and American newspapers reflect this daily. Three words are enough to hook the reader. The same holds true for advertising. Is it the French language's incapacity to be verbally economical that drives it to metaphor, visual exploration, and the realm of fantasy? While in the United States people tend to remember a jingle or a tag line, in France the public more easily recalls the image of 200 sheep that forms the Woolmark logo, or Nescafé's small train in the Andes. The French forget ad slogans.

This explains why in France there is an old and deeply rooted tradition of using posters. A poster can create only a visual shock. For decades, French art directors have not been layout designers or illustrators but the conceivers of ideas, in the same way that copywriters are in the United States. Thus, over half of French creative directors begin as art directors, whereas in New York 90 percent begin as copywriters.

In fact, the most distinct difference between American and French— and, indeed, European—advertising lies elsewhere. Europeans are more reserved, even shy. They hesitate to place their emotions in commercials. They fear slipping into sentimentalism. There is no fear of this kind in the United States. On the contrary.

Asked several years ago about English advertising and its so-called superiority, Mary Wells replied, "You hear a lot about that from Englishmen. While the British aim for cuteness and are sometimes funny, Americans have gone on to explore a lot of emotions like hunger, sex, fatherhood, etc. I think we are still 10 years ahead." True, Mary would have never admitted to being even a year behind. But it is also true that no one knows better than Americans how to seize and conjure up in a few seconds the feelings, the attitudes, and the desires of their compatriots. Remember Bill Bernbach's famous comment: "I can draw a portrait of a man crying and it will never be more than a picture of a man crying, but I can also draw it in such a way that it will make you cry." Bernbach agreed with Mary Wells. For them, American advertising is at its best when it creates emotions. They believe great advertising is "people" advertising. The kind of advertising that, at its best, touches the viewer like no other advertising in the world.

Some years ago in France, we created a surprising commercial for Hertz. Vultures were attacking a broken-down car on a deserted, windswept road. The attack was fierce. The car fell apart into a thousand pieces. The  commercial was at once hair-raising and highly competitive. In an article I wrote at the time, I explained that this commercial "is a typical example of what we are looking for. On one hand, it has everything to seduce those who favor the emotional—the vultures, the car breaking apart, the yellow ribbon tied around the Hertz car that drives up. It is quite a spectacle. But we are far from the purely spectacular. The audacity serves the product's hard (even hard-core) and extremely competitive discourse. The competition is symbolized by the vultures. From an idea that belongs to the realm of the imaginary, we managed to make a very competitive, product oriented film."

To show how competitiveness can be combined with the spectacular, I often refer to that famous Pepsi commercial, in which an archaeologist and his students in the year 3002 examine relics from earth: a guitar, a baseball bat, and a bottle of Coca-Cola covered in mud. Once the bottle has been cleaned with a laser, the archaeologist holds it up and one of his students asks him, perplexed, "What is it?" The seemingly well-versed professor simply responds, "I have no idea." For me, as for all Europeans, this commercial reconciles the "hard" and the "soft" sell so well. It is simply a masterpiece. The soft sell is the story, and the humor, and the hard sell, the film's extreme competitiveness. Americans have made their mark over the past 20 years, from Volkswagen to Nike, with masterpieces of this genre. Advertising is an applied art and, in these cases, Americans master it better than anyone.

Europeans adore the Pepsi ads—especially "The Archaeologist." But when it came out, the American marketing writer Martin Mayer said, "This is a pleasant piece of entertainment, and probably worth Pepsi's money because it makes the bottlers feel happy, but it is of course an inside joke for people in the advertising business and the cola wars." Then he added, "European Pepsi drinkers who saw the joke may perhaps have felt reinforced in their choice, but it's hard to imagine an American to whom this commercial would have sold a bottle of pop."

His commentary shows that the gap that exists between Americans and Europeans is not about to go away. I'm not sure Europeans are entirely wrong. On the European side of the Atlantic, people like advertising. In France, 65 percent of people declare themselves "publiphiles," in other words people who like advertising. Maybe this is the fruit of all our efforts to make them like what we do. In France, at the same time as we sell a brand we sell the act of advertising itself. By contrast, over two-thirds of the American public declare themselves "publiphobic" and view advertising as an insult to their intelligence.

The French actress Isabelle Huppert once said, "Americans have everything. They need nothing. They certainly envy our European past and culture, but in reality, we appear to them as an elegant Third World." For Americans, the world often stops at the water's edge. Creative work from London or Madrid doesn't seem to raise general interest in the United States.

Inspiration should be able to go both ways. If we believe that we must "think local" but keep our aims global, it is useful to try to understand the particularities of other countries. So let's leave the United States for a few pages to see how countries create, step by step, their own advertising culture. Let's start with Japan.

Japan

Though everything seems completely different at first glance, similarities do exist between the Japanese and the French mentalities. The Japanese constantly combine relentless technological progress and the conservatism of a highly traditional society. This duality is not foreign to most European countries. Behind their cool facade, the Japanese have a constant need for added cultural value, a "spiritual supplement," if you will. As much as the French, but in their own way, the Japanese are suspicious of the harshest aspects of the Western system.

In advertising, the Japanese share the French attraction to allegories. For more than a century, ads for Seibu, Parco, and Shiseido have demonstrated this. A poster created for Seibu, a Japanese department store, that shows a six-month-old baby swimming underwater is very revealing. The picture is superb. Just under the top edge of the poster, you can see the sur-face of the water. Beneath that, the open eyes of the swimming baby. The rest of the photo is filled with beautiful blue water and carries the caption "Discovering yourself." This ad was placed on all the streets of Tokyo as well as on a huge, 60-square-meter storefront. It was actually the poster to announce Seibu's re-launching. For the Japanese, nothing is more natural than a theme such as "discovering yourself," illustrated by a photo of a swimming baby, to promote the reopening of a store that has just been entirely revamped.

There is also a profound graphic tradition in both France and Japan. In Japan, writing by ideogram leads to the conceptualization of ideas through signs and symbols. This requires a long learning process, which completely shapes the minds of young Japanese and explains why, when they later become ad executives, they value the search for signs. They embrace the symbolic approach. Similarly, French advertisers often refer to the best French posters as ideograms. For them, a good poster is an idea expressed in images. There is thus a certain parallel between French and Japanese ad writing, based on the use of symbols and visual metaphors.

In Japan, writing for commercials is less matter-of-fact, less single-minded than in the West. They use countless inserts showing scenes from nature—sunsets, birds flying on the horizon, reeds bending in the wind. These scenes are integrated, in totally unexpected and illogical ways, smack-dab into the middle of a commercial on a completely different subject. For the Japanese, a rapid string of images constitutes for them a meaningful sentence, while for us Westerners, it's nothing but fast editing. Japanese advertising functions by the simple accumulation of signs. And if, for Sony and Nissan, it seems judicious to integrate an element from nature to counterbalance the impression of overindustrialization, why not do it?

Japanese advertising is not simply emotional. It taps into the richness of the imagination. And that's why it seduces us so much. Perhaps what we see there is a demonstration of what American sociologist Edward Hall calls the contexts of poor and rich. For Hall, the United States is an example of a country in a "poor" context. Thought frames reality; the subjective, the nonquantifiable, as mentioned earlier, is considered nonexistent. In a melting pot, the smallest common denominator creates a connection and permits assimilation, but by consequence weakens the context. In contrast, societies in "rich" contexts, such as Latin, Arab, Asian, and African countries, are more impregnated with a climate that surrounds everything. They are immersed in their pasts and saturated by their motivations and cultural foundations. One doesn't hesitate to take diversity into account or to see the complexity of human interaction, even if it is simply for commercial ends. In that milieu, people understand each other in "half a word."

The French expression *se comprendre à demi-mot* is difficult to translate into English. It literally signifies "to understand each other in half a word." Essentially, it means "to understand each other without having to spell things out." A kind of shorthand develops for people in the same culture.

United Kingdom

"Half-words" are second nature in Great Britain, the country of understatement. British creatives have established a real complicity between advertisers and their audiences. They have always approached business with a gentlemanly distance. I once commented to a Brit that advertising people should put more intelligence in their work. To which he replied with that typical disdain, "Put intelligence in business? I do believe there is nothing more vulgar." The English cultivate storehouses of intelligence to seem as if they have none.

In the United Kingdom, people believe that a message too easily understood is one that is trivial, banal. They say that the message is "on the nose" or "pedestrian." The day may come when we will see only commercials that make us wonder why they were made. The English may fall off the edge into the indecipherable.

That being said, for the last 20 years London has been the Mecca of advertising, the reference for creatives throughout the world. The British *Art Director's Annual* is read, reread, and dissected by creatives and even planners from every continent. This is due to Britain's great creative agencies: CDP, BMP, Saatchi, BBH, GGT, and Abbott Mead and to the exceptional generation that cut its teeth in advertising before graduating to Hollywood: Alan Parker, Hugh Hudson, Ridley Scott, Adrian Lyne, and others. But, most of all, the United Kingdom's preeminence results from this incomparable distancing, the capacity to act with an air of total detachment, all the while maintaining complete control over things and people.

Spain

Farther South, in the country of Goya and Almodóvar, one might assume that advertising is hot-blooded and overdramatic. Guess again: If it burns at all, it does so with more conceptual fire than blind passion. For the Spanish, selling a refrigerator requires no commentary; demonstration is enough. The immaculate machine is planted in a brilliant desert. A hand opens the door, takes out an egg, and breaks it on the top of the fridge, where the heat cooks it in two seconds. The name *Zanussi* appears on screen. Spain makes a specialty of unexpected demonstrations and visual unforgettables. This country discovered advertising late in life. Since the death of Franco in 1975, Spain has ogled England and the United States while keeping its Latin sense of the idiosyncratic. The result is one of the most creative countries in the world, where ad executives, working on limited budgets, prove the truth of the old axiom: Lack of funds spurs creativity. Somewhere between the elliptical and the intimate, Spanish advertising expresses its violence in a few strong images. And most often stops there. Which lends it an unsettling simplicity.

Germany

German advertising assumes responsibility for being advertising. Even more than their American counterparts, German ads seek exclusively to sell. They strive to convince, with a Protestant spirit that veers toward the austere. In the country of machine tools, Germans have a hard time admitting that the life of a product can be strongly influenced by advertising. That being said, attitudes are changing. In a recent commercial for Mercedes, a man comes home late and apologizes to his wife with an embarrassed, even guilty, air. He invents a story about his car breaking down. His wife slaps him immediately: A Mercedes never breaks down. Springer & Jacoby, the agency of Mercedes and others, is beginning to get the conservative German public to loosen up. Here and there, sudden spells of creative epiphany are appearing, such as the ads for Lucky Strike and the German railway. The country that we often caricature as being rational is also the country that invented romanticism. It will soon be a place where more than purely factual and reasoned advertising will sell.

Asia

Continuing this trip, we would notice how Norwegian advertising, with its crazy, random humor, is the counterpoint to the austere and strict style of neighboring Sweden. Or how Thai ads stand out against the general trends of other countries in Southeast Asia. In Bangkok, advertising people are defining their own style by going back to the roots of their own culture. Perhaps this is because Thailand is the only country in the region that has never been invaded by a foreign power—another example of advertising reflecting a country's culture and history.

In the Far East, and especially in northern Asia, advertising is gradually freeing itself from Western ways of thinking. There is a humility and a humanity that give messages a very particular sensibility. A commercial for China Motors features a peasant who, in the middle of a storm, journeys across kilometers of rice fields, his sick child strapped to his back. The voice-over is that of the son, who, having later succeeded in business, comments throughout the commercial in a touching tone, "When I was a child, I had a high fever. There were no doctors in our village, so my father had to carry me on his shoulders for miles and miles. Now that I'm older and successful, I can say to my father, 'Dad, let me carry you. . . .' " For its corporate message, China Motors evokes an eternal value, Confucian filial piety.

Ads are the mirrors of societies. They reflect their respective cultures. But, too often, we reduce the differences to mere stereotypes. How many times have I heard it said that American ads are simple-minded, English ads humorous, German ads boring, French ones too "executional," and Japanese ads esoteric? The differences are, in the end, more subtle and profound.

Advertising is often allusive. Each country talks to itself through hundreds of 30-second commercials, which offer glimpses of its collective culture. A country's uniqueness expresses itself here and there, like brushstrokes on a canvas. Globalization changes nothing. On the contrary, the more sophisticated advertising gets, the more advertising takes on local colors. Faced with an increasingly uniform world, each country strives to preserve spaces of freedom, oases of resistance, and cultural particularities. Each wants to continue to communicate within itself, as the English do so well.

Herein lies the advertising agency's challenge. We dream of every brand we work on becoming global. For a brand's image to be identical from one country to the next, we know we must take each country's specificities into account. We must be quick on our feet, clear-minded enough to know when we can do the same thing in different countries. And when we cannot. And we must be careful not to reduce everything to the lowest common denominator.

It is in this spirit that we created *Disruption*. Disruption strives to get the best out of each brand and how it manifests itself within each culture. It's a language of change. A common language that creates communities of thought beyond borders. It structures our network horizontally, transversally. It enables two account executives from two different countries, despite the distance, to understand each other when they talk of advertising strategy in a "half-word."

PART I

THE ROAD TO DISRUPTION

Part I explores how we came to Disruption and shows that its foundations lie in two spheres: the collective experience of the past 20 years in advertising and the nature of change in the business world at large. Therefore, the first two chapters, "Retrospective" and "Discontinuity," serve as our departure points.

2

RETROSPECTIVE

DISRUPTION IS A way of thinking. It's a marketing and advertising methodology. Its name implies the idea of rupture, of nonlinearity, a before and an after in the life of a brand.

Disruption was not born just like that, in an instant, by following someone's sudden spark of inspiration. Disruption is a fruit of our advertising past and of our collective experience. A fruit that has taken many years to ripen.

There is a relationship between the "great ideas" of the 1970s and the 1980s and what Disruption strives to attain. Disruption is a direct descendant of those ideas. That's why this first chapter is a flashback, a retrospective on "great selling ideas." This trip back in time is instructive. We will see that, if there is no leap, there's no idea. That a leap is a rupture, a discontinuity. The idea of disruption is already there.

But let's not move ahead too quickly. Let's return to selling ideas and to Procter & Gamble, the company that encouraged its agencies to create the largest number of them.

For a long time, I have admired a particular British advertising executive to no end. While today Tim Davis is not recognized the way he should be, in the early 1980s he was responsible for making Young & Rubicam London one of the best agencies working for Procter & Gamble in Europe.

I remember two commercials in particular that he had created at the time: one for Crest toothpaste and one for Flash, a household cleaning product. "It's not creative unless it sells," goes the old Benton & Bowles adage. Seen in this light, the Crest and Flash commercials are very creative indeed. These two brands, following the introduction of these new commercials, enjoyed a gain of market share over six straight Nielsen rating periods. If my memory serves me correctly, Crest gained 20 percent in only 18 months. Moreover, at the 1982 festival in Cannes, Crest received a Silver Lion and Flash was awarded a Bronze. It is not every day that award-winning commercials are business builders.

Still today, I vividly recall the Crest commercial. It is an animated film with an educational approach. A child's drawing appears on the screen showing Crest in the form of an eraser "erasing" the plaque from a little boy's teeth. Then other children's scribbles portraying their colorful renditions of brushing with Crest multiply on the screen. We're finally told that Crest is "fighting to make tooth decay a thing of the past." This spot is both instructive and entertaining at the same time.

The ad for Flash is based on a demonstration. It shows a 30-second close-up of a pair of glasses. The left lens, which had been scrubbed with scouring powder, is scratched. The right lens, cleaned with Flash, is sparkling, immaculate. What could possibly lend itself better to a side-by-side comparison format than a pair of glasses?

When these two commercials came out, I was head of Young & Rubicam's Paris agency. I felt a true sense of admiration for what Tim had accomplished. All advertising executives working on Procter dream of attaining the double honor of being recognized both by consumers (and in turn the most demanding advertiser in the world) and by advertising award festival audiences, even though the second offers fewer concrete benefits.

By the end of 1983, however, Procter & Gamble parted ways with Young & Rubicam throughout the world. It was a big blow. Procter & Gamble has always been the advertiser of every agency's dreams, the most sought after and prestigious client around. There are very few markets in which this company's brands do not rank first or second. The marketing science of Procter & Gamble remains unrivaled.

Six weeks later, at the beginning of 1984, Jean-Claude Boulet and I left Young & Rubicam in order to form BDDP with Marie-Catherine Dupuy and Jean-Pierre Petit. A few months later, Tim Davis and Chris Wilkins, his creative director, left Y&R as well.

Idea and Execution

Together with its various agencies, Procter & Gamble has, over the years, built up an advertising philosophy, or perhaps I should say an incomparable body of knowledge.

For instance, I remember one presentation, developed by the Compton agency in 1972 (now Saatchi & Saatchi New York), about 12 ways to conduct "real people advertising." It covered everything from the hidden camera setup in a Comet demonstration, in which housewives' reactions were captured live, to the editing of Ivory testimonials whose deliberately awkward style reinforced the feeling of authenticity. These presentations revealed a high level of expertise. Those were the days when Milt Gossett was about to become head of Compton. Agencies, especially Compton and Grey, had accumulated a great deal of useful experience and had managed to transform it into incomparable know-how.

This expertise was developed both at the executional stage and at the idea level. From an execution viewpoint, everything that makes a commercial more effective had been found out step by step. From then on, the problem/solution approach was favored. Demonstrations weren't supposed to be laboratory experiments but tests you could easily perform at home. The product had to be in use in the commercial. The situation had to center on a conflict, in addition to being believable. Every format (slice of life, testimonial, announcer, endorsement) was dissected, evaluated, and weighed once and for all. The good word on executions was being preached the world over.

At this point, it's useful to distinguish between an idea and an execution. The *idea* expresses the benefit in an engaging, distinctive way. The *execution* is the way the idea is presented, explained, and depicted (and not the way an ad is produced). Its role is to enhance the idea. An execution is an idea about the idea. In other words, the selling idea dramatizes the benefit, and the execution dramatizes the idea.

Ideas should be judged by themselves, regardless of the form their execution takes. Once we begin to judge the ideas behind the execution, we notice that many of the creative ideas for Procter brands are smart and insightful. It is time their brilliance is acknowledged.

Over time we all have, consciously or not, created our own advertising halls of fame. Mine includes 10 or so P&G selling ideas. It's a nice collection of oldies. But goldies.

Great Selling Ideas

There are a multitude of registers and innumerable sources of inspiration. If we are observant, everyday life reveals thousands of customs, habits, and reflexes. Little things we steal from people, as an artist would, and which provide an inexhaustible source of inspiration.

Among selling ideas, there are several great classics. Ideas that have been around a long time. Here are some blasts from the past.

Charmin is a brand of toilet paper whose thickness makes it highly absorbent. So thick, and therefore so soft, that most housewives can't keep themselves from squeezing it when they pull it off the shelf in the supermarket. This reflex inspired the idea for the commercials that feature an aisle manager who is overwhelmed by the disorder left by these women constantly touching the items. When he begs them, "Please don't squeeze the Charmin!", he is actually singing the praises, in an unexpected and original fashion, of the thickness of the product and thus of its high level of absorbency.

Gleem toothpaste is effective in preventing cavities, but no more so than its competition. In order to differentiate it from the rest, the ad simply stated: At work, you cannot brush your teeth after every meal. You need a toothpaste with long-lasting protection. Gleem's selling idea, "For those who can't brush after meals," is extremely shrewd. Showing that

Gleem fills a gap implies superior product performance: greater effectiveness in preventing cavities.

Babies crawl. And they often crawl in the kitchen, the most frequented room in the home. So the floor had better be spotless. That's where Spic & Span got its "clean enough for babies" idea. It makes the product, and especially the promise of cleanness, less banal. There's nothing harder than trying to find a new way of saying "clean."

Men aren't the only ones who sweat. Women need effective protection, too. They need products that are as effective as those made for men but with a different level of acidity. "Strong enough for a man, but made for a woman," is Secret antiperspirant's claim.

Nothing is more immediately noticeable than dandruff. It makes one look unkempt. Head & Shoulders has the good sense to remind us that "You don't have a second chance to make a first impression."

Sure invites you to raise your hand if you're sure. Folgers is the best part of waking up. Clinch makes cleaning as easy as dusting. Downy makes clothes as soft as feathers. And Gain gives you a sunshine clean.

Thanks to their potency, these ideas have stood the test of time. Most of them are at least 10 years old, some are older. Some are still on the air, but even those that aren't, such as Gleem and Charmin, remain ingrained in our memory. Inspiration came from the combination of observing daily life and understanding the "product experience." It is this marriage that enabled these brands to suddenly stand out in the crowd, to be seen differently. We can't look at Head & Shoulders without thinking of first impressions, we can't see Secret without thinking "strong enough for a man, but . . ." These selling ideas are *ownable ideas*, and these brands succeeded in claiming them as theirs.

A great selling idea exists in and of itself, regardless of its execution. And that's precisely where the beauty of it lies. One could even say that the stronger an idea is, the more it is separate and distinct from its eventual execution. It exists before its concrete expression. Usually, it is formulated in a cluster of words that speak immediately to the imagination. They add life and depth to the benefit. They go beyond the benefit, at once encompassing and enriching it. Evoking the idea of "first impressions" is much more compelling than pointing out that the product cures dandruff. The selling idea makes the brand a part of our daily lives. In some respects, the brand becomes inescapable. It has singled itself out.

Often, the claim is an exact translation of the selling idea, but not always. Coast's campaign claim was "the eye-opener," whereas the selling idea was "the smell that wakes you up in the morning." The selling idea actually represents the core of the message. It is what the story line tries to dramatize. Another excellent example of this is the old Crisco campaign, with the statement that accompanied the demonstration: "All the oil comes back, except one tablespoon." This was not the claim but rather the very foundation of the story. It was the selling idea.

It's worth our while to look a bit more closely at the Crisco ad. A woman, after having fried some food, puts back one spoonful of oil—only one—so that the level of the oil in the fryer goes back to its initial level. This is a perfect example of preemption. The idea's power lies in what it manages to imply: With a competing brand, it might take two, three, or even more tablespoons of oil to make the same amount of fries. Crisco's demonstration, in fact, transforms a performance attribute that is invariable from one product to the next into a relative one.

Relativizing performance is of capital importance. I remember working on a campaign for a dish-washing liquid that had a sheeting effect: Glasses washed by hand were free of streaks thanks to this sheeting effect that caused water to glide instantly off the glasses, taking the minerals with it. We could have made the promise "no need to wipe dry." It would have been involving but too general. A competitor could have then claimed the same benefit if he were to develop a similar product. But promising better grease-cutting action introduced the notion of different degrees of performance. Convenience is absolute, performance is relative. Which explains why convenience strategies should be ruled out.

I don't know who invented the expression "selling idea," but it's especially apt. We have to find ideas that, at the very least, sell. But they must also go beyond the short term and be capable of attaching themselves to the brand for the long haul. Ownable ideas enrich brands and increase their asset value.

We can name a few other great classics in addition to Procter & Gamble's: Maxwell House's "good to the last drop" or "Brush your breath with Dentyne," and the celebrated "melts in your mouth not in your hands," from Treets, now M&M's. In this last case, the idea's strength enabled it to slide smoothly from one brand name to another. That's the ultimate proof of the force of the idea. When these selling ideas have such power, they're an incomparable asset. I admire the creatives who came up with them. They may not be in the Advertising Hall of Fame but they deserve recognition.

The Creative Leap

What do Head & Shoulders, a shampoo, Sure, a deodorant, and Crisco, a cooking product, have in common? All three deliver. They produce an end result. They are products whose benefits consist in providing the consumer with a performance, unlike clothing, for instance, which makes people feel in vogue, or a soup, whose quality is tasting good. Does that mean that advertising based on selling ideas is limited to performance products? Not at all.

I remember producing a campaign for Jil underwear that said, "so soft, you can't help touching them," and a campaign for Liebig soup that said, "so good you can't help getting other people to taste it." (In passing, this "so . . . that" logic eventually became too much of a habit.) Neither Jil nor Liebig is, in the strict sense of the word, a performance product.

Orangina, a carbonated orange juice–based beverage, isn't, either. There has always been an unappetizing deposit at the bottom of a bottle of Orangina. But this deposit in fact proves that Orangina really contains orange pulp; thus, it's a sign of its quality. Hence the selling idea: "You have to shake a bottle of Orangina, to stir up the pulp." Orangina produced a great number of commercials to illustrate this idea. A bartender who is mechanically shaking bottles of Orangina and doesn't realize when the waiter hands him a bottle of champagne. Obviously, the cork flies off.

A ski-acrobat-turned-waiter at a mountain café performs incredible feats to keep his tray flat so the bottles of Orangina don't topple. His flips and somersaults end up shaking the Orangina. In more recent commercials, the Orangina bottle is anthropomorphized, but the message stays the same. Two men dressed as Orangina bottles are sent on a roller-coaster ride. Once they've already been shaken up, they're told they have to go again. In another commercial our Orangina men find themselves in a Nintendo game, following Super Mario as he jumps over various obstacles. The Orangina campaign is among the most famous in France. It draws its force from turning a product liability, the orange residue that settles at the bottom of the bottle, into an asset. The pulp becomes the proof of Orangina's natural ingredients. The campaign further synthesizes and conveys this message through the idea of shaking.

The shaking idea serves as a springboard for all the commercials. Its strength is what enables them to be so diverse. Here again, the idea exists independently of its dramatization. It can exist on its own.

Sometimes we criticize a commercial or a print ad for being devoid of an idea. What does that mean? After all, we've seen 30 seconds of images, noise, words, and music printed on a slice of film—in other words, a creative product. That's because we can't discern the thought that is hidden behind the images and sounds, even though it is supported by the components of the ad. The ideas for Charmin, Gleem, and Orangina actually exist beyond the elements that make up their commercials. There are a hundred ways to illustrate "don't squeeze the Charmin," "for those who can't brush after every meal," and "you have to shake Orangina."

When an idea is clearly visible, it magnifies the benefit contained in the strategy, that is, softness for Charmin, long-lasting protection for Gleem, and natural ingredients for Orangina. The idea enlarges the benefit.

The idea does not limit itself to being the literal expression of the strategy. It does not stop there. It carries with it a rupture, an invention, a leap in relation to the strategy. Hence the term *creative leap*. The leap measures the distance covered between the strategy and the idea, between softness and "don't squeeze," between natural and "shake me, shake me."

When BDDP opened its doors in 1984, we made the creative leap concept popular among marketing and advertising people in France. Aside from Orangina, the examples of campaigns having creative leaps that I referred to most during that era were the campaigns for Maxwell House and Heineken.

Watch someone make a cup of instant coffee. More often than not one starts by taking a spoonful, then, without thinking, goes back to the jar and, in a movement of uncertainty, rounds off the amount already put in the cup. Then one scoops up a little bit more, even if it means shaking some back into the jar from the spoon, hoping to make the coffee stronger so that it tastes more like real coffee. Quantity supersedes quality. This is what inspired the idea: "With Maxwell House, there's no need to add more. One spoonful is enough."

In Great Britain, Heineken's idea, as most know, is that "it refreshes the parts other beers cannot reach." In this campaign's first commercial ever, an announcer unveils the results of his experiment. After a long day of walking the beat, some policemen are invited to drink a Heineken. Once they've removed their socks and shoes and rolled up their pant legs, they drink their beer with utmost dignity. The announcer then closes in on the object of this experiment: the policemen's numb,  swollen toes that gradually come back to life. They start to wiggle. This becomes the proof that Heineken really does refresh the parts that other beers cannot reach.

Heineken's other commercials push the idea of refreshment even further. In each commercial, a Heineken goes exactly to the point where the drinker most needs it: The ears of a pianist are refreshed, the arms of some galley slaves row faster, William Tell gets a better grip on his crossbow, Nero's thumb is activated so he can indicate whether or not a gladiator should be pardoned. . . . More than 40 such commercials were produced. In a later one, for example, a wilting plant that is watered with Heineken suddenly comes to life. Similarly, a judge wearing a wig suddenly finds his hair starting to grow again after he gulps down a can. Each commercial conveys in its own way the same idea. Each one makes the creative leap longer. Each one strengthens the idea.

The Heineken and Orangina ads have been on the air for more than 20 years, and Maxwell House for 15. In the United States, Frank Perdue has been telling us "it takes a tough man to make a tender chicken" for two decades. Head & Shoulders, Secret, and Folgers consistently base their advertising on the same selling idea. The stronger the ideas are, the more mileage they get. More specifically: The stronger they are, the more they inspire numerous and varied executions. The diversity of executions pre-vents the campaign from wearing out. Better still, their very number and variety reinforce the ideas themselves.

Let's return to the notion of the creative leap: Although it looks as though it's nothing other than an idea, its interest lies elsewhere. In fact, it makes us better at identifying ideas that are false. An idea exists only if there is a leap. Otherwise, all you have are clever reformulations and repackaged strategies which, without the addition of a real idea, are not powerful.

Many campaigns do not contain a real idea. They settle for simply con-veying the strategy by combining words. When you scratch the surface to find the idea hiding behind the slogan, you realize that there is no idea. The very triteness of the theme usually precludes the use of strong visuals. Because campaigns like these settle for being the mere translation of the strategy, the simple visual expression of words, their limitations show up almost at once: The visuals are bland and shallow. They lack the spark contained in the Orangina and Heineken commercials, in which the ideas are brought to life by the images. An idea that isn't there is easier to see than to read.

The creative leap goes further. It gives us a new way of looking at and talking about a product. We end up somewhere else without knowing exactly how we got there. Something we had never paid attention to suddenly triggers a new way of thinking, and the idea sticks. It could be Maxwell House's "extra spoonful" or Head & Shoulders' "first impression." The change is such that viewers find themselves unexpectedly looking at a product from a completely new angle. Once the Orangina and Heineken campaigns had been aired, people never looked at these brands the same way again. Orangina is not jut a bubbly orange drink anymore; it's first and foremost the drink you have to shake. Heineken isn't just a beer, it's a beverage that refreshes body and soul.

Creative leaps are a way of recycling products: They are given an added dimension. Thanks to a creative leap, something that was once mundane becomes noticeable. Suddenly, these leaps make the product stand out. There is a before and an after in its advertising history, a discontinuity. The notion of a creative leap foreshadows the idea of Disruption: the notion of a break, a rupture, that constitutes the subject of the following chapters.

Leadership Advertising

The creative leap approach not only helps to better sell the client's products, it also gives people a tool to better understand the way a campaign functions. It helps planners and account people to identify and validate real ideas. It also forces them to write solid and innovative strategies. To make a leap, you need a springboard. An inspiring strategy acts as a launchpad.

On an operational level, however, the creative leap has proved too limiting when interpreted word for word. Some great campaigns, such as "Coke is it," "This Bud's for you," and "Don't leave home without it," seem both brilliant and effective without necessarily being founded on a leap. Their messages are nothing more than a translation of their strategies. They follow a different system of logic. They are leadership campaigns.

What do we mean by *leadership advertising?* It is an inseparable and harmonious union between a prominent product and advertising that comes across as being equally important. It is created by brands that have succeeded in attaining an unrivaled standing: Coca-Cola, AT&T, Budweiser, and others. Their advertising has to avoid the risk of being inadequate. It has to be "as big as the brand." In the end, the force of their advertising matches or even surpasses that of the product itself.

This type of campaign usually has a certain resonance because it picks up on popular lifestyles or trends. Coca-Cola is more than just a carbonated thirst quencher. As early as 1945, it became the very expression of a way of life. Club Med is more than just a resort; it's a means of rediscovering oneself, of reinventing an entirely new "me."

Nowhere do these advertisers say "we are number one." They are never explicit about their leadership status. Their campaigns manage to make you feel they represent prominent brands. They promise the world. Or, as one client told me one day, "they consider the universe above them rather than the competition below."

Leadership campaigns are too broad to be specific. But they are far-reaching. Nike and Hallmark, for instance, each have created their own languages. By having their own particular styles of expression, they make it more difficult for their competitors to attack them. The issue is no longer "Is my brand the only one that can stand behind this campaign?" but rather "By using this campaign, will my brand become a reference, and thus give my competitors less room to maneuver?" Actually, this is category advertising. But it's done on purpose.

By being omnipresent, a leading brand reduces all the more the space in which its competition has to move. It narrows each competitor's possible advertising venue. In Europe, brands such as Danone, Evian, and Nescafé have been presenting themselves as leaders for a long time. Their competitors are then left with a smaller share. The tone of a leadership campaign contains the simplicity, power, and serenity that make the target of the message think they're hearing a statement of the obvious: The product was made for them. It's theirs. This effect has been attained by Dim and Kronenbourg in France, by McDonald's and Levi's in the United States, and by British Telecom and Sainsbury in the United Kingdom.

Leaders must speak more often to the heart than to the head. Kodak, AT&T, and Singapore Airlines have become masters of the art of the emotional. Here we have come a long way from problem/solution and side-by-side formats. The advertising wants to be likable. It pulls the audience in. For 20 years, the commercials of the U.S. Postal Service and Hallmark—not to mention Mean Joe Greene for Coke—have moved all of America. The land of pragmatism and positive demonstration is also the land of *coups de coeur*, or impulses guided by the heart.

One question logically follows: Is leadership advertising for leaders only? The answer is no. A challenger, even an outsider, can decide to portray itself as a leader. This can help bring it success more quickly. In advertising, a book often can be judged by its cover. Apple understood right from the start that no brand could exist in its sector without being big and without being perceived as an institution. As early as 1984, Steve Jobs bought all the advertising pages of one issue of *Newsweek*. More significantly, he made the "1984" commercial into an event. Pepsi, too, acted the leader in anticipation of the future it cast for itself. What could be more assertive than declaring oneself "the choice of a new generation"? The blatant optimism of the Pepsi campaigns leaves no room for doubt. Pepsi presents itself as a leader. It claims to be at the front of the race to win the hearts of the new upcoming generation.

In fact, the issue isn't really whether the brand is a leader or a challenger. The main thing is knowing if a brand should raise its sights and take on a broader, more encompassing discourse, proportionately reducing its competitors' capacity to react, or if, on the contrary, it should get back in the ring, stop being assertive, and adopt a competitive, even comparative, discourse once again. Whatever the brand, you have to decide if you will speak either as a leader or a challenger. It seems to me that this is the first question that should be asked.

Idea–Territory–Value

How can what's been said about the creative leap be reconciled with observations on leadership advertising? They appear to come from wholly unrelated spheres, as though advertising was made of distinct worlds.

As we will see, the goal of Disruption is to bring them together. Before developing the Disruption methodology, we used a conceptual tool that grouped brands and their campaigns into three categories: ideas, territories, and values. Orangina and Head & Shoulders belong to the first, since their advertising is founded on an idea (a selling idea, or in other words, a creative leap). Levi's and Marlboro exploited a territory. Nike and Apple fell into the third category because they embodied a value. Grouping campaigns in such a way proved very fertile. In our examination of the creative leap, we have discussed ideas, selling ideas, at length. Now let's be more specific about what we mean by territory and value.

Territory

"Come to where the flavor is," Marlboro used to say. According to the dictionary, a territory is an area that falls under the jurisdiction of an authority. In advertising, it's a set of signs that a brand creates and is then recognized by. The advertisements for Marlboro appropriate a territory as symbolized by the famous cowboy, with weathered skin and blue eyes, looking off toward the horizon. People identify with his rough-cut style. He is a symbol of virility. He brings the brand an imaginary added value. Similarly, Levi's personified the 1960s "Berkeley" generation. Its territory was casualness and rejection of authority.

In 1961, Procter & Gamble bought Monsavon from L'Oréal in order to establish itself in France. Ten years later, Procter stopped investing in this declining brand. Its market share had dropped to under 2 percent. Then the brand manager took the initiative to return to the original, outdated, old-fashioned packaging. Sales took off. The product went back to its original quality, simplicity. Its commercial featured a young woman with dazzling skin that breathes health who told the camera: "I don't even do anything complicated. I wash my face with water and Monsavon. I like it because it's simple, with milk, a bit of lavender. And it leaves my skin very clean. And that's the first thing I ask of a soap." The voice-over ends with "Monsavon is simple. It respects a skin's fragility." Monsavon refound its original territory, that of simplicity. Today, Monsavon is the market leader.

No one has made use of territories more than perfumes. They appropriate them, whether it's sensuality, escape, eroticism, seduction, exoticism, violence, baroque, classicism, country life, or even surrealism, as Chanel did in the United States by inviting us to "share the fantasy." For the last 20 years in Great Britain, Benson & Hedges and Silk Cut cigarettes have stood apart from the herd by using a surrealist register.

In the first few years of its existence, in France, BDDP created two territory campaigns of note: Rodier and Porto Cruz.

Rodier, a ready-to-wear brand of clothing considered a little too classic, wanted to rejuvenate its image and target a younger crowd. We decided to portray the new, modern women that writer Françoise Dorin described as wearing pants by day and skirts by night. In other words, a woman who refused to define herself according to exclusively masculine criteria. One such woman, in the confusion of an airport whose employees are on strike, said, "Stuck at Charles de Gaulle. Too bad for Jimmy. Lucky for Henri!" as though she were not overly upset with her misadventure. Another, in the middle of her ransacked apartment, exclaimed, "Me jealous? And how!" A third, walking past a cluster of workmen who whistled at her, declared, "There'll be hell to pay the day they don't whistle!" Rodier had chosen its territory and tone. For the first time in fashion, women were depicted with real personality and sense of humor.

Tibet is the land between earth and sky. Basque country is the place where strength is a virtue. The sea, too, has a country: Greece. The way these countries poetically depict themselves sparked our idea for Porto Cruz. It became the port wine that comes from "the country where black is a color." The territory of Porto Cruz is authenticity. No other brand invokes Portugal with such eloquence.

Marlboro, Monsavon, Benson & Hedges, Chanel, Silk Cut, Porto Cruz, and Rodier are brands that managed to define their own territory. They established a specific place for themselves, indeed, a dominant place in brand geography. They take up lot of space in our imagination. They can't be uprooted.

Value

A brand can claim a territory. It can also take on a value. This brings us to our third register.

Phil Knight described Nike's advertising by saying, "We show competition, determination, achievement, fun, and even the spiritual rewards of participating in sports activities." The Wieden & Kennedy commercials for Nike are famous, but as far as I'm concerned, the ads that gave birth to the Nike saga were those produced by Chiat Day. One in particular was filmed in a single shot with a fixed camera. In the distance, a man is running. Then he leaps forward, right toward the camera. It is Carl Lewis, whose feet, after a 30-second, slow-motion jump, land in the sand and fill the screen. Carl Lewis's voice can be heard saying: "My first jump was a joke. Nine feet. But I said to myself, 'Don't give up.' In high school, I kept coming in second. I could have quit. But I believe that you should never give up. When that's your philosophy, there's no telling how far you can go."

The idea of surpassing oneself was born. Physical exertion was glorified. From then on, Nike embodied a value. Wieden later bolstered that value's impact by ordering us to "Just do it."

A few years ago, Printemps, one of France's leading department stores, came out with a campaign that was very ambitious. It decided to tell everyone that they should rely more on their emotions. To give them free reign. A department store is a place of freedom, escape, and discovery where people go to get a whiff of what's in the air, to wander, to enrich the senses. Compared to this, the hypermarket seems like a rigid place, the incarnation of a purely rational world. The Printemps press campaign sought to intensify feelings. The visuals were juxtaposed in unusual, surprising ways in order to trigger an emotional shock: a woman's arms crossed like the legs of a horse, eyes gazing off in the distance bringing meaning to train tracks that disappeared on the horizon, two hands crossed like the leaves of a hardy plant. The theme of the "A meeting with emotion" campaign made Printemps the place of everlasting emotions. Printemps wanted to be at the heart of all that was felt.

In France, Darty embodies trust; Hachette, enthusiasm; and Michelin, rigor. In the United States, Apple expresses liberty regained; Pepsi, youthfulness; Oil of Olay, timeless beauty; Saturn, the American competitive spirit; and AT&T, the promises of the future. These brands know how to raise the level of the discourse. They are a bit like the heroes of our era. The values they embody are the stuff heroes are made of, to the point of a car maker, Porsche, adopting the motto: "The race against oneself is the only race that's never won."

Idea. Territory. Value. The idea is usually conceptual, territory is most often sensual, and values are emotional. In other words, an ad speaks to the mind, to the senses, or to the heart. With these three registers, we cover all the ways to talk to a human being through advertising.

Idea and Thought

Placing an idea opposite a territory or a value would seem to imply that campaigns founded on a territory or a value do not contain an idea. That's partly true. When Ralph Lauren advertises, all he has to do is say what he's about and what he wants to embody. An updated style of old New England. He has a territory. When Nike urges us to surpass ourselves, summoning us to "Just do it," it is not basing its advertising on an idea but rather on an opinion in the form of advice. If there are ideas, they are usually executional ideas that each commercial represents. But they are not the overall concept of the campaign. Actually, territories (such as New England) and values (such as outdoing oneself) are often specific. The brands that personify them, such as Ralph Lauren and Nike, appropriate them de facto. Unlike Orangina, Head & Shoulders, and Heineken, they don't need a creative leap to stand out. Being themselves is enough.

The idea-territory-value triptych served as our guide for many years. Initially, it allowed us to diversify our angles of attack, to diverge from having a creative leap in each of our campaigns. If there was no leap, we sought campaigns that were based on a territory or a value. By making this distinction we knowingly made exceptions to the creative leap principle. As a result, Porto Cruz, Rodier, Hachette, and Printemps were among the best-known campaigns we had done in France at the time, without being creative leaps per se.

Actually, rather than saying that territory and value are "idea-less" registers, we should say instead that they are based on thoughts. We can benefit from comparing idea and thought.

Orangina's shaking and Heineken's refreshing all extremities are ideas. Monsavon's returning to simplicity and Nike's encouraging people to surpass themselves are thoughts. An idea is an original solution, a discovery. An idea is perceived intuitively, instantaneously. However important the preparatory work may be, it is not enough to produce an idea, which implies a leap. It's only afterward, retrospectively, that the idea finds its justification. Edward de Bono refers to a "logical link-back."

A thought is grasped differently, in a reasoned and gradual fashion. It's a way of forming a judgment about something, an intellectual opinion. Several aspects have to be balanced, synthesized. New perspectives have to be opened.

We are impressed by a novel and potent *advertising idea*, such as "Refreshes the parts other beers cannot reach." Its astuteness draws us in. But we are won over by an *advertising thought*, by what it redefines and asserts, like "Just do it." An idea must strike the viewer, whereas a thought must persuade.

An idea can be great. But a thought is always beautiful.

3

DISCONTINUITY

LET'S TAKE A step back from the world of advertising to look at things from a different perspective. To realize that, in every domain, discontinuity is a source of progress. To understand that discontinuity is at the heart of Disruption.

If you've read or heard of *Rubyfruit Jungle*, *Six of One*, or *Rest in Pieces*, you're familiar with Rita Mae Brown. This writer is at once a novelist, activist, poet, translator, essayist, and scriptwriter. Through each of her works she battles stereotypes and rises up against intellectual laziness. In one of her books, she offers an incisive definition of insanity: "doing the same thing over and over again, expecting something different to happen."

People don't realize to what extent they always think in the same way. At some point, we all believe we have created something original. Most of the time, we haven't done anything new, just more of what's been done before, with perhaps a little personal touch. As a result, we are living in a world of sameness. Tom Peters calls it a "sea of similarities"; Jean Baudrillard, a "Xeroxed world."

Faced with this situation, companies understand that they cannot go on doing things as they've always done them. But without realizing it, they fall into another kind of conformity. To impose order on change, they plod down the same worn paths. A kind of organizational panurgism has taken root. And all of that leads to a world of utter equalization.

As Edward de Bono said, "Restructuring leads to business reengineering. Cost cutting to downsizing and outsourcing. Quality and service policies to benchmarking." Conformity and repetition prevail. The will for change itself has become banal.

Even when justified, reengineering makes the mistake of leading people's energy and mind-set away from the essential goal, that of finding new ideas and creating ruptures. Benchmarking, too, has its own limits. While benchmarking does measure a company's competitiveness product by product and helps it to regain lost ground, it in no way enables a company to project itself into the future or to shape its business. Systematically, a company that benchmarks is always one step behind. Benchmarking is the opposite of discontinuity.

After we have restructured, reengineered, and rediscovered the importance of the client, what's left? What enables something different to happen? What's left is what makes the real difference: creativity. Creativity as the tool for change.

In a world of hypercompetition, we can no longer use the same old recipes. We must abandon our habits and stop being afraid of what's new. Stop being afraid of change, and start banking on creativity. More precisely, we need to understand the relationship between the two, that creativity is a way of managing change.

Change is Discontinuity

There are two ways of imagining a brand's future. The first path to the future is drawn from one point to the next; the intended destination is known from the start. You extrapolate a trend. In the second, the final destination is unknown. You move forward step by step, day after day, guided by your idea or your vision of a brand. Every day you adjust your actions to fit the ups and downs of the economic situation and of the competition.

Although the second path is less reassuring, it's the only sensible, the only viable one. For the very idea of extrapolation is the root of fatal errors. Even with a healthy margin of error factored in, an extrapolation rarely turns out to be exact. The future is rarely a mere projection of the present.

In *The Age of Unreason*, Charles Handy describes the age we live in as one in which "the only prediction that will hold true is that no predictions will hold true." In his view, even change itself has changed: "Change used to be more of the same, only better, but not anymore. Today, change is discontinuity." In other words, change no longer follows a pattern. That is why we must start thinking upside down, backward and forward, inside and out.

No incremental answer will suffice. Yet many companies still foster a culture of incrementalism: a little product improvement here, a little line extension there. Making a few simple adjustments gives them the impression of being reformers. They create an illusion of change. But in fact, change is the opposite of incrementalism.

All business-book authors have emphasized this in their own way. It's become a leitmotif. In Charles Heller's eyes, the environment is only partly predictable, so "you need discontinuous strategies that are novel and based on creativity." According to Michael Hammer, "Every company is replete with implicit rules left over from earlier decades." He believes that strategic planning should serve to expose and then jettison these out-of-date rules and assumptions. For Robert Thomas, "The degree of discontinuity is the extent to which the firm makes a departure from the market needs." Edward de Bono sees "lateral thinking" as a way to get off the beaten track. All these authors strive to get out of the common line of thought. They all preach discontinuity.

There is a very fine line between a common ground and a common-sense observation that's worth making. Discontinuity is an illustration of this. Many people talk about it, but few are brave enough to face the consequences. Most of the time, discontinuity inspires far-reaching revisions in a company's culture as well as in its way of seeing the world. A kind of reprogramming. Discontinuity creates change.

Reversing Perspectives

In the business world, and especially in the stock market, uncertainty is unpopular. That is why businesses are often uncomfortable with the idea of discontinuity. It is seen as an unsettling irruption of the unknown. And yet, beyond this sphere of business, discontinuity can be a fertile way of thinking.

Our century has witnessed the collapse of Continuist thinking, the heir to the cult of progress and Positivism of the nineteenth century. This collapse occurred in all fields, from natural history to the history of sciences to artistic creation.

For many years, the very idea of continuity in nature has been questioned. Darwin's theory of evolution was riddled with missing links. Life on earth probably evolved in fits and starts, by upsets in the balance of things. When Voltaire said it was wrong to assume that "nature doesn't make leaps," he showed great foresight.

What is true for nature has proved true for science as well. The history of science was merely an accumulation, a continuous search for perfection. Newton's flawless equations provided a glimpse of the future the moment one took the past into account. Since then, the theory of determinism has been leveled. In fact, every age has its own academic science, which contains a set of tacit conventions that in turn form a paradigm. Then, one day, an anomaly appears in this paradigm that forces people to search for a new explanation.

A discovery brings more than increased knowledge. It displaces an entire network of knowledge. There is nothing incremental about it. The discovery of oxygen made it necessary to invent the modern chart of chemical elements. Maxwell's equations led to Einstein's theory.

Each time a lens is refocused or a perspective overturned, a qualitative leap is sparked. We see, for the first time, what was always right before us. After Copernicus, new stars appeared. After Galileo, all of nature's pendular movements were suddenly visible. The list is infinite. Stephen Hawking and the big bang, the revolution of fractals in physics, the paradoxical research in immunology made necessary by viral epidemics, and so on. By reversing our perspective, these ruptures give birth to new visions.

If there is one field in which discontinuity is a constant, it's modern art. The birth of the avant-garde is considered to date back to about 1907, when Picasso painted his *Demoiselles d'Avignon*. Until then, artists and the public had the feeling they were part of a blossoming story. There was a continual pursuit to create paintings that perfectly imitated nature itself. Starting with the Renaissance and the invention of perspective, the aim of painting was to provide the truest possible representation of reality. Art was figurative. Reproducing was required. Then with modern art, breaking with aesthetic conventions became the aspiration. Jean Cocteau said, "Beauty is being produced rather than reproduced." Like the movements that followed it, Cubism made a spectacular break with the earlier dogma of representation. Each new avant-garde movement—abstract art, surrealism, expressionism, pop art, and so on—exposes a once-unspoken convention and goes to great lengths not to change it step by step, but to destroy it in one fell swoop. In music, the basic convention of traditional composition, the scale of tonality, was mercilessly abandoned by composers such as Schönberg and Berg. In literature, narrative continuity, even grammar itself, were blown apart by Proust and Joyce. Every avant-garde movement takes an opposing stance to that of the one that preceded it. Umberto Eco, the Italian semiotician and sociologist who became known to the general public through his novel, *The Name of the Rose*, uses a vivid expression to describe discontinuity: *cogitus interruptus*.

These examples come to us from on high. It is always worthwhile to seek inspiration from the very top. If today many are concerned that advertising, in New York and elsewhere, runs the risk of becoming a commodity business, maybe it's because they don't try hard enough to question established ideas. People don't realize how many conventions the market has created.

Advertising has only slightly evolved since the creative revolution orchestrated by Bill Bernbach, David Ogilvy, and Mary Wells in the late 1960s. It has gone the way of continuity. Although their world was the scene of some veritable ruptures, today, many great agencies have become conservative. The time has come for them to humbly but resolutely draw inspiration from the great minds of the times, be they artistic or scientific. Unlike many people in advertising, these cutting-edge thinkers are inherent questioners, unafraid of change.

Business Discontinuities

When I was 10 years old, I could recognize a Cadillac or a Thunderbird by its taillights alone. Those days are gone. Today, a Peugeot 305 looks like a Renault 9, an Infiniti like a Pontiac Bonneville, and a Honda like a Mitsubishi. From one company to another, the same consumer studies have led to the same conclusions, and thus to the same products.

However, exceptions do exist. A growing number of companies have become aware of the dangers implicit in such standardization. They are trying to develop products that constitute a rupture with what the competition has to offer. These business discontinuities come in three forms. First of all there are *technical breakthroughs,* like those made by Sony or Canon. Then there are *additions,* those big or little things companies decide to do, or add, to differentiate themselves and their brands from their competition. Nordstrom, in the United States, and Tesco, in Great Britain, are examples of this second type. Finally, if the company is having too much trouble coming up with a breakthrough, and if it is unable to strengthen itself through one or more added ideas, it can nonetheless try to develop a different viewpoint and share it with the public. It thus adopts a new stance, or *posture,* that is new in relation to the market or to itself. Here again, it creates a discontinuity.

Breakthroughs

Sony is the epitome of discontinuity. It sees all its competitors' accomplishments merely as conventions to be overturned. "The public does not know what is possible, but we do," Akio Morita used to say. If Sony has managed to attain an exceptionally high rate of success in its new product launches, it has done so by constantly anticipating the needs and desires of its customers. Most of its new products have been discontinuities with regard to both the competition and the previous generation of Sony appliances. Apple developed computers that spoke the language of man and spurred the revolution of the PC over the monolithic mainframe. Canon capitalized on its expertise to develop personal copiers with the quality standard of photography. Within just a few years, Canon was competing with office copiers by Xerox. Xerox then had to face the risk of becoming to photocopying what mainframe computers are to data processing. Lotus changed the face of business when it introduced 1-2-3, the first spreadsheet. It did the same 10 years later when it embraced the concept of Notes technology.

In technology-driven markets, innovations are discontinuities. From one product generation to another there is usually a technological leap. Especially in computers, copy machines, cars, and aeronautics, these leaps jump out at you. The Chrysler minivan was "the right vehicle for the right time" and has lured customers into Chrysler showrooms where they hadn't set foot in ages. As for 3M, it has created a technological discontinuity practically every week since its inception with products such as Post-its and Scotch tape.

It's easy to conclude that technological breakthroughs are the exclusive domain of a certain category of companies—that is, generally, those that market consumer durables. When you think about where breakthroughs occur, you rarely think about categories such as, for example, food. Here, most people think, the novelty lies in recipes and packaging. This is a mistake. Take Whitbread Breweries in the United Kingdom. For years, they strove to use technology to create a competitive edge. Their achievement, a patented can with a special pressurized mechanism that gives canned beer the taste and creamy texture of draft beer served in pubs, was the discontinuity that  gave birth to Boddingtons. Whitbread's "cream of Manchester" is now one of the most popular beers in the United Kingdom and proof that even in the beer market, change can be technologically driven.

Danone's Bio yogurt is another proof of innovation in the food cate-gory. The cultures found in Danone yogurts were first imported by Daniel Carasso in the 1920s. Since then, the cultures have been carefully kept alive to the point where the importance of preservation far outweighed that of innovation. That is until Danone decided to breed new cultures. The results of that change are Bio yogurt with active bifidus, which im-proves intestinal transit time, and Bio with active Caséi, which strength-ens the immune system. In France, Danone now sells 50,000 tons of Bio every year.

Another good example of innovation in the realm of food is probably Snickers, which became the number-one-selling frozen snack in the United States in only five months. It's one more proof—and certainly not the least impressive—that great innovations take place in the food arena.

And what's true for food applies to other categories as well. While countless other clothing companies settle for trying to keep up with fash-ion's random trends, Levi's literally reinvented pants by creating Dockers, a product halfway between jeans and dress pants. Levi's version of the classic chino was new and different because it embodied a new lifestyle, much as jeans had 20 years earlier. Those people who believe that product discontinuities and technological innovation are limited to consumer durables or packaged goods are mistaken. Dockers is a case in point: It al-ready represents 20 percent of Levi's worldwide sales.

Additions

If you can't *innovate*, you can *add*. There is a famous story of the angry cus-tomer who brought a pair of tires back to Nordstrom. Although tires have never been sold at Nordstrom, the purchase was reimbursed. What better proof of Nordstrom's commitment to the satisfaction of its customers? This is just one of hundreds of anecdotes, true or invented, that have built the store's reputation for top-notch service. Nordstrom customers often trade "shopping at Nordstrom" stories, each trying to have his or her tale be more unbelievable than the previous one. The explanation for this is simple: The service really is incomparable. A Nordstrom salesperson advises you in your selection, helps you try things on, takes care of alterations, wraps things up, helps you check out, handles returns, and even follows you from one department to another. Therein lies the novelty: You can be dressed from head to toe by the same salesperson. This is why Nordstrom has become the most closely watched, if not the most copied, chain of stores, not just in California, not just in the United States, but in the entire world. Of all my French clients who are in retail, not one has failed to spend at least a few minutes in a Nordstrom store. Obviously, when you add something, you have to pay for it. Nordstrom does employ more people than its competitors. However, its so-called overstaffing has paid off: Over the last 15 years, its sales have increased sevenfold.

Home Depot, too, created its point of difference through its salespeople, who have all, in a former life, been craftsmen of one sort or another: carpenters, plumbers, gardeners, electricians. When you talk to them, they give a less anonymous impression than do salespeople in other large stores. They have not lost their passion for their original profession. More important, they make a point of sharing it with their do-it-yourself customers.

Tesco, one of Great Britain's two largest companies in the food retail industry, has made additions the heart of its policy. The very theme of its advertising is "every little helps." At Tesco, consumers can exchange products they purchase with no questions asked, mothers with small children can reserve parking places close to the front doors, kids are looked after by staff while their mothers shop, extra personnel pack clients' bags, stores are now open late on weekends, and ready-made meals are available for the hurried working person, and so on. Tesco has even opened what it refers to as "metro convenience stores," which, as their name implies, are located in commuter rail stations. Today, Tesco has climbed into first place for the first time ever and boasts over five million holders of the newly launched Tesco Fidelity Card. That is the power of tangible ideas.

Addition-driven discontinuities are not just found in the realm of service. They can be created at the product level as well. For instance, both

Häagen-Dazs ice-cream and Starbucks Coffee developed stores that are more than simply places for serving coffee and scooping ice cream. Rather, they are places where the customers have the feeling, and rightly so, that they are buying more than just products—they are buying an experience.

Ben & Jerry's premium ice cream, since its inception, has expressed its socially conscious bent by donating a fixed percentage of the sales of certain flavors to specific charitable organizations. Rainforest Crunch's proceeds help preserve the world's rainforests, whereas sales of Peace Pops and Brownie Bars benefit the Children's Defense Fund. Sales of Cherry Garcia, named for the rock legend's favorite flavor, goes to his brainchild, the Rex Foundation. The by-product of Ben & Jerry's important social contribution was the creation of its unique point of difference. In 1994, the Walker Research Foundation found that 50 percent of American consumers were willing to pay a price premium for products whose companies were viewed as socially responsible.

If creating a genuine breakthrough appears impossible, you should concentrate on finding a complementary idea, something extra. When you do that as well as Häagen-Dazs and Starbucks have, you create a veritable discontinuity. Häagen-Dazs revolutionized the ice cream market with its stores just as Starbucks did the coffee market.

Add or subtract, which is what IKEA did when it eliminated salespeople, as did The Body Shop when it got rid of excess packaging. In both cases, as in many others, successfully subtracting an element brought about a new vision.

Thus, technology-oriented sectors do not have a monopoly on discontinuity. Far from it. Along with Sony and Apple, we can name Boddingtons, Starbucks, Tesco, and Nordstrom. Some have actually invented something new, in the strict sense of the term, while others have added an element to an existing product or service. But in the end, all represent real progress for the consumer.

Examples like these speak for themselves; yet there are not millions of them. Too often, a particular product or service is considered to be untouchable. We don't ask whether we can add something new. Instead, we content ourselves with selling the product or service "as is" and relying on advertising to enhance the value of the brand. We forget that the sign of a strong brand is its constant commitment to improving its product.

Posture

What path do you follow when creating a breakthrough or adding something new turns out to be impossible? Is this reason enough to give up on discontinuity? No. The discontinuity may lie elsewhere. It may be found in the posture that a company or brand adopts.

A posture can be either brand driven or market driven. When a posture is brand driven, the brand acts as if its view of itself will become the reference for the market. Its posture is created from the inside out. By contrast, when the brand assesses the world around it and, as a result, transforms itself, its posture can be said to be created from the outside in.

From the Inside Out   The Gap represents a rupture with the competition. Without having created a breakthrough or adding anything new, The Gap simply saw its market differently: from the inside out. And that was enough to create a discontinuity. The Gap got consumers to buy the idea that unobtrusive clothing actually enhances a person's own unique look. It created a trend of antistatus style that comes from wearing basic, no-frills clothes and it made it chic not to make an effort to be chic. The Gap stood for antifashion fashion. And while this is not an easy stance to maintain, The Gap has been managing quite well for almost 20 years.

Through its creation of Saturn, GM succeeded in seeing its business in a new light. Its top management realized that the future of Saturn depended as much on the spirit of its employees as on its product. Saturn adopted a highly discontinuous view of the car industry. It rejected the Big Three affiliation and it acted like a start-up, with the objective of producing cars that were competitive in both price and quality with Japanese cars. Dealerships were transformed into "stores." Fixed pricing allowed both salespeople and customers to talk about the car instead of the price. Above all, Saturn made its customers feel like part of a new movement, a return to American greatness.

Ever since deregulation, airline companies have been engaged in merciless battle. Pan Am and Eastern have fallen by the wayside. Airlines observe and copy one another constantly. But progress is only incremental, as, for example, with Continental's BusinessFirst and TWA's Comfort Class.

Then came Southwest, which systematically follows a path different from its competitors'. Its fleet is composed exclusively of Boeing 737s; having a single airplane model reduces training time and inventory. Southwest has no connecting flights, only round-trips, which enable it to avoid the hub-and-spoke system. This allows Southwest to use the gates it rents in various airports with much higher daily frequency. Taken separately, these discontinuities would not have made much difference, but applied together, they have made Southwest the greatest success story in its sector. Its rates are lower by a third than its competitors'. Recently, Southwest's founder and CEO, Herb Kelleher, commented, "Everybody has expectations, preconceptions, whether from schooling, training, or conventional wisdom. Then, they encounter the real world and it just doesn't conform. . . . So everything I was taught has no validity whatsoever."

The Gap, Saturn, and Southwest envisioned their respective sectors differently. They looked at their industry with a fresh eye.

From the Outside In Looking at oneself from the outside in, rather than from the inside out, can prove equally productive. When a company examines itself, taking into account the outside market, and comes to see itself in a new and different light, the results can often be astonishing.

For years, Oshkosh sold only overalls for adults. Until the day when the company management realized that there was also a demand for sturdy, hard-wearing clothes for children. Today, children's clothing represents more than 90 percent of Oshkosh's sales—a great transformation, thanks to this company's recognition of an unexploited market opportunity and a brand-new perception of itself.

In 1974, Interstate Department Stores was on the brink of bankruptcy. Sales were plummeting. It had lost its raison d'être. When you're a young

CEO working in an organization that sells items from 15 different sectors, it's almost unthinkable to abandon 14 of them. And yet that's what Charles Lazarus did. He got rid of all Interstate's discount stores and the majority of its department  stores and focused on its most original and prof- itable concept, which he had created only 10 years earlier—toy super- markets. Lazarus' vision of his company's future was discontinuous, to say the least. Interstate died. And Toys "Я" Us was born.

Intel understood that a subcontractor, too, can be a brand. By inform- ing consumers that the microchip is as important to the computer as the brain is to humans and that Intel stood for superior brainpower, Intel en- couraged consumers to make "Intel inside" a primary buying criterion. Be- cause Intel presented itself differently, buyers saw Intel in a new light.

Anyone can take a new road. When basketball showed that it is not just a sport but the symbol of the American competitive spirit, everyone suddenly became a basketball player. A participant, not an observer. And when you consider, or more appropriately, listen attentively to country music, you realize that country is no longer about middle-aged stars in tacky costumes singing "white man's blues." Country music artists saw the need to return to the genre's simpler roots, to sing about today's issues, and to write for a broader audience. Today, country is the United States' fastest-growing music segment.

Taking on a new posture can also be highly effective for consumer products. Alka-Seltzer and Schweppes tonic water are prime examples. Alka-Seltzer differentiated itself when it went from the fizzy headache medicine to the antidote for hedonists who had overdone it. Schweppes, the ultimate drink mixer, decided to enlarge its market definition and thus became the purely adult soft drink that's powerful and fulfilling "on its own." For both, the significant change in posture led to powerful results.

This can also happen for an entire product category. For example, shoes inherited a new status when jeans became more commonplace. Shoe brands now reflect teenage personalities the way jeans did before them. This is clearly demonstrated by Nike, Reebok, and Adidas on one hand,

and Puma, Keds, and Converse on the other. All these brands picture and position themselves differently. They adopt new stances, thereby creating breaks with the past.

Markets seem sedentary—rigid, so to speak—only until a daring brand or company shakes up the status quo. When it does so, everyone else is forced to follow suit. Often the end result of any kind of discontinuity, be it a breakthrough, an addition, or a change in posture, is the displacement of an entire category.

Breakthrough	Technologically driven	Canon Sony
	Nontechnologically driven	Boddingtons Danone
Addition	Service companies	Nordstrom Tesco
	Nonservice companies	Starbucks Ben & Jerry's
Posture	Inside out	The Gap Saturn
	Outside in	Toys "Я" Us Oshkosh

There is one company that, throughout its history, has managed to build discontinuity on discontinuity: Banc One. It pioneered the first technical *breakthrough* in banking by inventing BankAmericard, known today across the globe as VISA. Then it created a discontinuity through *additions* by being the first to introduce automatic teller machines and small, convenient branches in supermarkets. Given its unmatched history of innovation, Banc One was in a position to see itself as more than a simple bank, but a brand. Banc One has always seen itself differently. Its *posture* is reflected in its slogan, "Whatever it takes," which captures what all companies and brands should do.

Encouraging Change

To create discontinuity, you have to welcome change. While many pretend that their actions are motivated by this, the reality remains that they only give lip service to change. And at the end of the day, they don't practice what they preach. As Steinbeck said, "It is the nature of man, as he grows old, to protect himself against change, particularly change for the better."

Marketers are among those who are not the most daring. Over time, they create obstacles for themselves. They shape ways of thinking that prevent them from looking for change and push them to stay on the beaten track.

I could pick out several impediments to freeing up one's imagination. The fear of cannibalism is one of them. Often companies do not capitalize on new technologies they have developed. Instead they hide behind the excuse that introducing technological change would actually be detrimental to the current brands that they have. The same holds true for any new idea that could potentially shake up the status quo. This unspoken belief is often so strong that companies become willing to run the risk that a real competitor could exploit the very idea that they developed, or a new idea that came to them. They are so afraid of creating a discontinuity in their brand's life. They don't understand what, for instance, Gillette has been doing for years: consistently launching products that compete with each other. If you refuse to compete with your own brand, you end up standing still, not evolving. Launching a competitor to your brand is not depleting your assets; not launching one is.

Another obstacle lies in what some refer to as the "excessive cult of the consumer." Being "customer-driven" has become a common battle cry of American companies. As a result, many became misguided by the notion that being intimate with and understanding the consumer was the secret to success. But this is not always the case; there are limits to being consumer-led. After all, the consumer can't imagine the future any better than anyone else. For Barry Diller, former president of Fox Television, we remain "slaves to demographics, market research and focus groups." And he adds, "We produce what the numbers tell us to produce. And gradually, in this dizzying chase, our senses lose feeling and our instincts dim, corroded with safe action." If you ask consumers what you should do, which product you should launch, expect to get a conventional answer. The unquestioning respect for what the consumer has to say has, in fact, become an excuse for continued conservatism.

Perhaps the most significant barrier to change resides in our obsession with creating sustainable advantages. When a brand has built its clientele, when it has created a competitive edge that translates into market share, its natural reflex is preservation. It looks to safeguard its market share and hopes that the brand's competitiveness doesn't erode. Marketing vocabulary translates this way of thinking. For example, people talk about "ownable ideas" and "market preemption."

In his book *Hypercompetition*, Richard d'Aveni stigmatizes the attitude of those who think they can base themselves indefinitely on acquired advantages. For him, these people encourage the erosion of their company's innovation capacity. "Hypercompetition requires a fundamental shift in the focus of strategy," he declares. "Instead of seeking a sustainable advantage, strategy in the hypercompetitive environment now focuses on developing a series of temporary advantages." This necessity of always being one step ahead holds true in more than just technological markets. Trying to ensure one's stability and equilibrium is futile, and we will see this is true whatever the sector: packaged foods, consumer durables, financial services, and so forth. The acceleration of change has made the desire to maintain the status quo a moot point. Anachronistic.

These are just some common beliefs that drive safe action, that have become anchored in the minds of each of us and have been perpetuated by a certain fear of the future. There are certainly others. Together, they reflect a growing uniformity of thought, which, in turn, impedes innovation and risk taking.

For risk to be reinvented, it must be seen as a catalyst for change. In one of his books, Tom Peters quotes Steve Ross saying that "people get fired for not making mistakes." It's a wonderful comment. Risk taking implies accepting the possibility of failure. It is that freedom that can turn anybody into an entrepreneur.

This is why the head of a company must encourage people to let their energy flow, enable them to give their imagination free rein, to have the guts to leap into the unknown and invent discontinuities. An entrepreneur is simply someone who is more daring than others. Someone who likes to incite change.

Four American university professors have studied change in a book entitled *Marketing Masters: Secrets of America's Best Companies*. They found that successful companies have one thing in common: "They see change as an ally, a force not to be feared but to be welcomed and exploited." The Body Shop, Starbucks, Microsoft, Barnes & Noble, and Fox Television know that it is not enough just to adapt. Such companies create change in their markets. They write new rules of competition. They understand that change is an engine for growth.

> **"The world moves faster than thought.**
> **Yet only thought can make sense of the world."**
> **J. P. Barbou**

Today, companies either manage their markets or their markets manage them.

The Blackadder Metaphor

I have a particular affection for Blackadder. Who is Blackadder? He is the hero of a British television series starring Rowan Atkinson in the title role. One episode, entitled "Blackadder Goes Forth," recounts a new version of the First World War and acts as a metaphor for what we all should avoid.

First Officer: "Now, Field Marshal Haig has formulated a brilliant new tactical plan to ensure final victory in the field."

Blackadder: "Ah, would this brilliant plan involve us climbing out of our trenches and walking very slowly towards the enemy, sir?"

Second Officer: "How can you possibly know that, Blackadder? It's classified information!"

Blackadder: "It's the same plan that we used last time, and the seventeen times before that!"

First Officer: "E-e-e-exactly! And that's what is so brilliant about it! It will catch the watchful hound totally off guard. Doing

	precisely what we have done eighteen times before is exactly the last thing they'll expect us to do this time. There is, however, a small problem . . ."
Blackadder:	"That everyone always gets slaughtered in the first ten seconds?"
First Officer:	"That's right. And Field Marshal Haig is worried that this may be depressing the men. So he is looking to find a way to cheer them up."
Blackadder:	"Well, his resignation or suicide would seem the obvious way."

In this world of accelerating change, this clip emphasizes that we must resist applying the same models over and over again. That's easy to say and even easier to agree on. But even among those who share this point of view, many would contradict it the instant they are faced with a new and challenging problem. Their reflex then would be to take a familiar route. To fall back on an already proven solution. Stouthearted attitudes too often give way to fainthearted behavior. It's a long way from attitude to behavior. The familiar instills confidence, the conventional reassures.

Brands, companies, and agencies must constantly battle this tendency and force themselves to overturn ready-made ideas. Unlike Field Marshal Haig, we all need to open our eyes and find a freshness we have lost. Looking for discontinuities in advertising is a way of doing just that.

PART II
THE DISRUPTION DISCIPLINE

Discontinuous change at the company or product level does not happen every day. That's where advertising comes into play. Part II demonstrates how Disruption in advertising can be the catalyst for change that touches all facets in the lives of companies and brands. The chapters entitled "Disruption," "Convention," and "Vision" are the heart of the book and demonstrate how advertising can become a tool for change.

4

DISRUPTION

"ON JANUARY 24, 1984, Apple launches Macintosh. And you will see why 1984 won't be like 1984." That was the voice-over of the film that launched Macintosh. The allusion to George Orwell's novel made this an unforgettable commercial. The advertising approach was as revolutionary as the product itself. With the Macintosh campaign, Apple added an advertising discontinuity to a business discontinuity.

In fact, business and advertising discontinuities have different natures. Business discontinuities will, more often than not, have a greater impact than advertising discontinuities. When the Polaroid camera and the Walkman came out, these products were so revolutionary they created new markets.

Yet product discontinuities such as these are rare. All the more reason to look to advertising to create one. To do whatever it takes to bring about a new phase in a brand's life. To make people "reread" the brand, and to help them see it with fresh eyes.

Once we've seen the commercials for Lexus and Infiniti, we'll never look at Japanese cars the same way again. Ever since the Pepsi challenge 25 years ago, Pepsi has become the choice of each new generation. The moment the Energizer campaign broke the mold by claiming "Still going . . . It keeps going and going . . ." Duracell ceased to be seen as the unassailable leader. People now believe that nothing outlasts the Energizer battery.

IKEA didn't settle for claiming, "It's a big country, someone's got to furnish it," it educated Americans that lower prices did not mean lower quality. When Federal Express declared, "When it absolutely, positively has to be there, overnight," the face of delivery changed. Overnight. From that point on, people expected things to get done in a flash. After California Milk, we realized that milk was something we couldn't do without. Then there's Jell-O, one of the most predictable, ordinary products around. That is, until an advertising campaign took the country by surprise when it recast Jell-O as the eight-calorie dessert.

In the life of each of these brands, there was a before and an after. There was a break. There was a discontinuity. A discontinuity that resulted from advertising. A disruption.

Disruption: What It Is

When you look at the advertising landscape throughout the world, you notice that advertising disruptions are rare. A large number of advertising campaigns are predictable. They conform to a norm. They merely deliver, in a more or less creative way, a message whose content can hardly be considered original.

Discontinuity in advertising occurs when both the strategy and the executions are ruptures with what has gone before, when the planner rejects using a familiar approach and the creative does so as well. This, however, is not commonplace. The impression is that it just occurs now and then. Some of the time. You can't really tell how. More often it looks as if it happens by accident.

Finding ideas at random is not acceptable. We should not simply rely on chance or even on the creative's spark of genius. That's why we introduced a brand-new methodology. Its foundation is our refusal to settle for what's been done or said before. Its purpose is to make what all too often results from luck the fruit of a systematic approach. It's a sort of undisciplined discipline. We call it *Disruption*.

We define it in general terms: "Disruption is about finding the strategic idea that breaks and overturns a convention in the marketplace, and then makes it possible to reach a new vision or to give new substance to an existing vision."

This definition may sound a bit academic. We should always be wary of definitions. To *define*, in its etymological sense, means to "put an end to." In other words, to create limitations. That is the very opposite of what Disruption seeks to accomplish. Disruption is about displacing limits. Forcing them back.

Stratégie de Rupture

Disruption has been in BDDP's blood since its inception. What began as a *stratégie de rupture*—applied to many of our first clients, who brought us problem brands—became a mind-set that we realized could also be applied to brands not in decline. At the end of the day, there's no guarantee that a healthy brand will stay healthy. Unless someone finds a way of constantly renewing it.

In the May 1, 1992, edition of both *The Wall Street Journal* and *Le Figaro*, a full-page article entitled "Disruption" appeared. In it, we explain the central idea of our philosophy and our methodology: that the strategic stage demands imagination. And this is exactly what Disruption strives to encourage.

Breakthrough executions are not enough. With Disruption, we want to provide innovative thinking about our clients' brands before we even get to the stage of producing creative work. We need to become creative before the creative work starts. Great campaigns are always ruptures with the prevailing advertising language, not only in style but in content. Great brands are those that tell us something new. The issue is therefore breaking with conventional thinking at the strategic level.

With Disruption, we wanted to find something that would radically influence our clients' businesses. That would go further than any other advertising methodology. Without arrogance, but with determination.

Throughout our network, Disruption has become a shared mental model. Yet when we developed the Disruption methodology, I was caught between the desire to design an innovative strategic tool and the fear that any methodology might end up being paralyzing. I have always believed that predefined strategic formats are too prescriptive, too confining, that they slow down the imagination.

The answer was to perfect a flexible, open-ended system. One that would be more than just a method. A system that would create an attitude, a state of mind. In its usage, Disruption has proved itself very productive. It's a system for people who hate systems.

A Three-Step Process

Apple, Lexus, and IKEA represent more than a change in technique or style. They renew the content, the substance. They attack head-on prevalent ideas and deeply embedded habits. We have our own way of talking about it; we say that these companies have disrupted a convention, with a clear vision of where, as brands, they want to go.

We've taken this mind-set and turned it into a discipline. The Disruption methodology is a three-step process which consists of studying successively and systematically the convention, the disruption, and the vision, then, for each given problem, finding the link that will bring together the three notions, thus revealing how the vision refers to the convention that itself inspired the disruption.

The methodology's objective is therefore to define what share of the future a brand can envision and to find disruptive ways of accelerating that brand on the road to its chosen future.

Convention

The first step is to identify conventions. This is not as easy as it sounds. Although conventions are everywhere, they are generally hard to see. There are things that we don't even notice because they are so familiar. That's the force of habit. Depending on the case, we will talk about unquestioned assumptions, good old common sense, or the current rules of the game. In other words, conventions are those ready-made ideas that maintain the status quo.

It was conventional thinking to consider computers as being reserved for specialists. Apple questioned that assumption. It's conventional thinking that women should grow old gracefully. Oil of Olay challenges this every day. It's conventional thinking that retail advertising must be built on tangible elements such as product range and price. Virgin Megastore, the French equivalent of Tower Records, constantly defies that mandate by casting itself as the main promoter of youth culture, far from the domain of sales and promotions. Conventions, as we will see later in more detail, can be divided into three types: marketing, consumer, and advertising. Apple overturned a marketing convention, Oil of Olay reversed a consumer convention, and Virgin challenged an advertising convention.

Disruption

The second step is what we refer to as the disruption step. It is the one where, all at once, we question the way we have done things in the past. We discover that our way of thinking has been conditioned by biases. We realize that adherence to outmoded frameworks leads to creative work void of energy, and that the search for consistency is at the expense of creativity. Disruption precludes conservatism. It doesn't settle for the safe and the predictable. On the contrary, the disruption stage is about all-out questioning, about developing new hypotheses and unexpected ideas. It is a journey into uncharted territory, a quest for angles of attack that have never been used before.

IKEA dared to show that the intermediary functions of its competitors artificially increase prices. No salesperson, no delivery: That is a disruptive idea. In coming up with Saturn, General Motors showed a complete disregard for the widespread notion that American cars can't compete with Japanese cars. Saturn is special. And, thanks to Hal Riney, so is its advertising. In one of its commercials, an employee says: "You put a lot of yourself into something like this. You take all that enthusiasm and transfer that into the car. It all started with the challenge from the old values, to maintain the old values. . . ." Quite a disruptive way of selling a car. Saturn reconciles automotive modernity with enduring American values. It was exactly what was required, yet so unexpected. Another (and quite different) example is Bartles & Jaymes. These two grass-roots characters personified the authenticity of their brand. They portrayed their product as a truly wine-based beverage, breaking with the conventional positioning of the category, which tends to sell wine coolers as soft drinks for grownups.

IKEA, Saturn, and Bartles & Jaymes broke away from convention. They took another road—their own. In the following chapters, we will see dozens of brands that have gone against the grain: Nike, the NBA, Norwegian Cruise Line, Snapple, Sprite, *The Economist*, Levi's, Little Caesars, and others. All these brands differentiated themselves through advertising. Above all, they endowed themselves with a totally different brand meaning. They are more than competitive. They are unique.

Vision

We start with a convention, then try to find a way to disrupt it. But we have to remain true to the brand and to the way we would like people think about that brand. We therefore have to be very clear about the long-term brand vision. Formulating that vision is the third step.

The vision is a leap of the imagination from the present to the future. It's picturing where the brand will be over time. It's imagining the brand on a larger, more ambitious scale.

IBM decided that it no longer wanted to be seen only as a mainframe computer manufacturer; instead, it wanted to become the provider of "solutions for a small planet." *The Wall Street Journal* doesn't just give us the news, it gives itself the role of decoding the activities of the financial market that are so often incomprehensible: "Money talks. We translate." NASDAQ does not want to be seen as the second-biggest stock market in the United States, but rather as "the stock market for the next hundred years." For Intel, a microprocessor is more than a computer chip. Intel's ambition is for the whole world to understand that it's what's inside that counts. We will see that Virgin is not just the sum of its various businesses—record labels, music stores, airlines, and so on. It's modern youth's cult brand. As for *Forbes*, it not only acts as a news magazine, but more importantly as a "capitalist tool."

All these brands express, through their advertising, a fresh vision of what they stand for. Their campaigns single them out from the competition. Disruption can give a brand new life by giving it a new vision. It provides a glimpse of what does not yet exist.

Rethinking the Strategic Process

The Disruption methodology proposes an open-ended framework for approaching any strategic or creative issue. It focuses on the strategy both upstream at the company level and downstream at the advertising one. The convention/disruption/vision mindset can be useful to anyone in any domain—trying to find new product ideas, for instance. When we think in terms of Disruption in advertising what interests us is the vision toward which a company or a brand is striving and the way in which the advertising strategy and execution reflects that vision.

Disruption brought us to a point where the conventional approach to advertising strategy, the promise/reason-why duo, is of little help. The reason for this is simple: It is nearly impossible to think differently if you cling to the same conventional tools. Disruption's focus on the vision helps to move back upstream, thereby stretching the traditional advertising process. It encourages looking for a larger picture, which gives us a better chance of bringing more meaning to the brand, by renewing its vision.

Convention/Disruption/Vision is the strategic format implemented in each of our agencies. Here are two examples. The first is for Virgin Megastore in France:

Convention	New retail concepts should focus on the tangibles they offer: choice, price, services.
Disruption	Give Virgin an emotional role, rather than make tangible promises.
Vision	Virgin is not a record store, it is the temple of culture.

The second is for Clairol Herbal Essences Shampoo:

Convention	All shampoo advertising focuses on end benefit: beautiful, shiny hair.
Disruption	Dramatize the experience as a benefit in itself.
Vision	It's the refreshment and renewal of washing one's hair that makes one feel beautiful.

The Disruption format is each brand's strategic guide. It is the catalyst that drives the brand toward its vision.

Degrees of Disruption

After years of experience, studying, and creating hundreds of Disruption formats, I have found that it is worthwhile to distinguish between two main types of disruption: low level and high level. Low-level disruptions are those that result when attacking a convention leads to a renewal of the brand, not the market: The brand's place within a given market has been shifted as opposed to the displacement of the market itself. By contrast, high-level disruption occurs when the company, by expressing a new vision, displaces the entire market. We will see throughout the book examples of disruption: high and low, big and small. We will see that there is no correlation between the degree of disruption and a strategy's overall effectiveness. High-level disruptions are not more effective than low-level ones. It's not that simple. The market dictates what can, and often what must, be done.

Let's look at five of our own examples.

High-Level Disruption

Virgin

Virgin Megastore, located on the Champs Elysées in Paris, has become a cult meeting place where the young and hip convene. It is the largest record store in France. One might have expected, and rightly so, its advertising to be based on tangible elements such as price, selection, service, hours, and so on. For many, that is the only viable way to advertise a retail company.

Virgin does not subscribe to that point of view. Its campaigns do something totally different, almost outrageous. They use a voluptuously plump woman as a muse to embody the store's credo: We can never make enough room in our lives for music. The poster, designed like a record cover and followed by several others, helped make Virgin a cult name among French teenagers. The Megastore is not just a store but a temple to popular modern culture, street culture. The latest posters say "Virgin Megastore. Forget what you don't know" and, "Virgin Megastore. So culture will no longer be reserved for those who are cultured." Virgin went beyond its retail status and took on a role—that of being music's—and, by extension, pop culture's—greatest defender. No tangibles. A real disruption.

Oil of Olay

Skin-care companies are very conservative in the way they advertise, especially when they deal with aging. In *The Fountain of Age*, Betty Friedan points out how deeply everyone's conventions about aging are entrenched. "People are way ahead of the advertising," she writes. "There are no images of women over 30. Age is always defined as deterioration or a decline from youth."

So what are we to think of a skin-care company that no longer promises women they'll look younger? This breaks with the all-pervading orthodoxy.

In one of the commercials for Oil of Olay, a woman declares, "Yes, I'm 36. And if I see one more gorgeous 18-year-old trying to sell me wrinkle

cream, I'm gonna scream! There are so many beautiful women of all ages. . . . I think I'm beautiful." The commercial goes on to claim "A lifetime of beautiful skin."

"Advertising," adds Friedan, "is slow to come to grips with reality, that the complex reality of women, and age, might sell. It would be a real change but I think there is going to come a daring company that will try it one day." That's, in fact, exactly what Oil of Olay did. Today, Oil of Olay no longer stands for looking younger, but rather for being beautiful at any age. Aging is a natural part of life. Thanks to Oil of Olay, you're the best you can be at your age, whatever age that is. Overturning the traditional mandate of striving to look younger is a profound discontinuity. With the "lifetime of beautiful skin," Disruption was introduced into Oil of Olay's copy history.

TAG Heuer

In the last few years, a new brand has made a place for itself in the inner circle of prestige watches. This was not an easy task. Seven years ago, TAG Heuer was simply a sports watch. A great sports watch, but not a luxury watch. Sport and luxury were two different worlds. To upgrade the brand's status, it was necessary to offer a new perspective on what sports could embody. TAG Heuer demonstrates that in sports, as in any competitive activity, it is the power of the mind that makes the difference. By doing so, TAG Heuer enters the minds of athletes, each of whom creates a unique adversary in order to push beyond his or her own limit: a shark for a swimmer, a razor blade instead of a hurdle for a jumper, a stick of dynamite for the relay runner, a 50-story-deep abyss for the equestrian.

In essence, TAG Heuer redefines prestige. It is no longer about someone's purchase power, but rather about being the symbol of an individual's mental strength. Because we know that victories can be won by a hundredth of a second or by a few centimeters, and that things can happen in the blink of an eye, the power of concentration and, more important, the ability to surpass oneself are fundamental. Antoine Blondin used the metaphor that the quintessential sportsperson is one who is locked in a jail cell but who pushes the four walls back a bit farther each day. It's all about individuals against themselves. The disruption in the TAG Heuer campaign lies in its ability to marry two seemingly unrelated do-

mains: sport and luxury. That's what the celebration of mental strength did. TAG Heuer has seen its turnover more than double in the last five years. Among the brands that have two lives, before advertising and after advertising, TAG Heuer ranks well. Success is a mind game.

Low-Level Disruption

BMW

In France, BMW's products have an excellent reputation. The cars, manufactured in Germany, are believed to be sporty and well built and to provide high performance through advanced technology. BMW engineers are among the best in the world. They refuse to compromise on the quality of their vehicles, and impose their views on the market by building what Americans call "the ultimate driving machine." So BMW's product image is great. But the same cannot be said for the brand itself. Many people perceive BMW as being too inward-looking, too self-centered, almost selfish.

When you go from a product to a brand, you're moving from an object to a person. Agencies have been discussing brand character and brand personality for years. For them a brand is like a person. We can push this parallel even further and think of a brand as having more than just a personality, but opinions and attitudes as well. From this perspective, BMW would be rather condescending. It would talk down to people. It would be arrogant, even pretentious. The result: Consumers could feel rejected by the brand.

It's up to advertising to break out of this position, to reduce the distance between the brand and the public. If BMW is seen as too exacting and impersonal, the objective is then to give it a little more sensitivity.

The commercial is in black and white. A baby grimaces, clenches his fists, and lets out a wail whose meaning anyone can understand: He's hungry. The viewer catches his breath. He can't take his eyes off the  screen. Quickly, almost impatiently, a hand clasps the back of the baby's neck. It is the hand of the mother, whom we never see since the baby remains in close-up. Quickly, the hand draws the baby's head closer. We expect the baby to start nursing, but instead we watch his face, from the side and in slow motion, smash against the breast as against a plush cushion. The crying stops. The baby starts to gurgle happily and relaxes his fists. The viewer breathes a sigh of relief. A nursery tune accompanies the caption, "Remember the feeling of your very first airbag." Mother and baby fade. A car appears with the BMW logo. The entire ad has lasted 30 seconds. This was one of the most powerful spots in France in 1995. Undeniably, it left an indelible mark during the commercial break.

Another spot, also in black and white: A child is playing with a toy car. He vibrates his lips to imitate the *vroom-vroom* of a motor. The noise is exasperating, earsplitting. The child's father can't stand it anymore. His eardrums are about to burst. Close-up on his ear. A hand reaches for the child's car and replaces it with a toy BMW. The noise stops immediately. The child now plays in complete silence. On the screen the caption appears: "Sealed Engine, Turbo Diesel by BMW."

These two commercials, as well as the more recent press ads that coincided with the launching of the Series 5, added a new dimension to the BMW image in France. They managed to give BMW a more sensitive side and to put the brand more in touch with the consumer. They combine exacting standards with sensitivity. The black-and-white film, the harshness of the music, the close-ups, the abrupt editing, the car driving silently at the end, all this represents rigor. The mother, the baby, the child playing with a toy car—all humanize. For BMW, these ads are real disruptions. Thanks to them, the brand is much less self-centered.

Clairol Herbal Essences

Recently, Clairol decided to make its classic shampoo, Clairol Herbal Essence, one of the most popular brands in the 1970s, more suited to the 1990s. It did so by relaunching an entire line of shampoos, all as organic and natural as their precursor. Making an impact in an overcrowded category with limited financial resources required departure from conventional approaches in all respects.

Clairol's disruption was driven by a new way of looking at the product category. It understood that there was an opportunity to do something drastically different from the competition, which focused exclusively on the end benefit: beautiful, healthy, shiny hair. By demonstrating that the experience of washing one's hair can be an energizing and revitalizing, natural, simple pleasure, Clairol succeeded in claiming a unique territory that it could own: pleasure.

The translation of this disruptive strategy onto the screen was inspired by an unexpected source. If you've seen the movie *When Harry Met Sally*, you're sure to remember the scene in which Meg Ryan fakes an orgasm in front of Billy Crystal, in the middle of a crowded restaurant. As she tosses her hair, strokes her face and moans, "It's so gooood, ohhh, ohhh," he grows more and more uncomfortable. In the heat of simulated passion, she starts banging on the table. The camera pans to the shocked expressions of the onlookers. After observing this unexpected outburst, a middle-aged woman tells her waiter, "I'll have what she's having."

What could have as much impact and express natural pleasure more than taking Meg Ryan's celebrated simulation into the shower? A woman in the shower washes her hair with Clairol Herbal Essences. Gradually her face brightens, her movements become downright suggestive, and she starts to moan in a way that is anything but ambiguous. She's getting more and more turned on. After 20 seconds of this "totally organic experience," the scene changes. For 5 seconds we see, facing the camera, a disheveled young couple with lank hair sitting on an unmade bed, blankly staring at the television screen. Just as in *When Harry Met Sally*, the woman turns to the man and says, "I want the shampoo she's using."

It was the combination of a disruptive strategy and a brilliant execution that gave birth to a campaign that managed to gain impressive notoriety and boosted sales in a category where it was outspent four and five times over. For Clairol, necessity was the mother of a great disruption.

Virgin, Oil of Olay, and TAG Heuer, thanks to their new visions, displaced their respective markets. BMW and Clairol have totally renewed their images by attacking conventions about themselves and have, as a result, further entrenched themselves in their respective markets. The goal of Disruption, high-level or low, is the same: giving a brand new force and gradually making it irreplaceable. When we wonder what share of the future a brand can hope for, it's often useful to ask ourselves: What would happen if it ceased to exist? What would people miss? If the answer is "Nothing," there is real cause for alarm. We need a clear, precise, and concrete sense of what would be lacking. Otherwise, how are we to know what people are attached to?

Strategy and Action

Disruption is not a pretty word. Some even consider it ugly and clumsy. Let's say it is potentially controversial (just like any good ad). It might make you uncomfortable. But it conveys exactly what we want to do: Stir the pot, alter the rules, wake up the consumer and create change.

The idea of "breaking off" is contained within the word *disruption*, just as it is in *irruption* or *interruption*. The prefix *dis-* emphasizes this notion. It is even a kind of pleonasm, since *dis-* already indicates severance. From *dis*advantage to *dis*tortion, from *dis*tress to *dis*agree, *dis*appear, *dis*approve, *dis*believe, *dis*claim, *dis*connect, and *dis*order, the sense of breaking off is abrupt. Never more so than in *dis*credit or *dis*grace. In certain other words, however, such as *dis*continuity and especially *dis*cover, the prefix takes on a positive connotation.

The word disruption is sometimes used in English and in French to describe a sudden opening of an electrical circuit. This image is particularly apt. Inherent to disruption is a surge of energy. Unlike rupture, which is a passive acknowledgment, disruption is active. It strives toward a specific objective. It is at once strategy and action.

Some might say there is nothing new in the idea of Disruption. True, it's not an invention. It's more like a discovery. Similarly, advertising doesn't invent anything but rather brings into the light what was hidden. "You invent nothing," Socrates said, "you rediscover what you have forgotten." In fact, Disruption is the recognition of a pattern in previous successes: We try to formalize the principles that lie at the heart of today's greatest advertising success stories, our competitors' as well as our own. Like an athlete who mentally replays past performances in order to understand what made him or her win.

Disruptive Ways of Thinking

We said earlier that Disruption is about displacing limits. Forcing them back. Postdisruption, there are generally three different possible results. The brand is reframed; people see it differently. Or the brand is defamiliarized; people's interest in a brand is suddenly renewed. Or the brand is recomplexified; consumers see brand characteristics they had overlooked before.

Reframe

The concept of Disruption contains the notion of restaging, reshaping, reframing. Lexus reframes our idea of Japanese cars; Apple, our idea of computers; MCI, our idea of the telephone; Fruitopia, our idea of fruit juice flavors.

Great campaigns lead to a shift in perception. Suddenly, the brand is seen in a different light. The moment the "Lemon" print ad appeared, no one looked at Volkswagen the same way again. In the life of Avis, there is a before "We try harder" and an after. The first Benson & Hedges commercial featuring the disadvantages of long cigarettes enjoyed not a 24-hour but a 24-year recall.

Any product category has an overall image, made up of the cumulative effect of a given sector's advertising campaigns. Laundry detergents, for example, have their own image, as do banks, beer, and sports shoes. I'm not saying that all the ads in a given sector are similar, but rather that, taken together, they create a general impression. Then, one day, a brand comes along and breaks out of that mold. That is precisely what Sainsbury, in the United Kingdom, Nike, in the United States, and Danone, in France, have done. Their ad campaigns were new and powerful, and did more than simply strengthen the brand. They shook up the whole market and made consumers look at it differently. In the United Kingdom, Sainsbury forged the image of retail sales. Danone altered the way the French see dessert. Nike created a totally new perception of sports shoes the world over. When these brands speak up, they displace the entire market.

In *The Age of Unreason*, Charles Handy provided a colorful definition of this notion. According to him, "reframing is the ability to see things, problems, situations in other ways, to look at them sideways, to put them in another perspective, or another context . . . it means taking information, perspective, knowledge, and looking at them in a new light. It will materialize through a leap, a turning point, a transversal idea, you name it." Well put. By the way, that could also serve as a description of disruption.

Another good example of reframing. Coca-Cola is a brand that is and always will be simple. The Creative Artists campaign that was disparaged by so many is, in my view, an interesting model of reconfiguration. At first glance, the theme "Always Coca-Cola" is hardly original, and what's more, the numerous executions go off in every direction. Many of them are flat, even weak. But I've always felt that the diversity of executions was a strength.

More than any execution in particular, what's striking is the sheer number of them. This is a break with the brand's monolithic tradition and its rather lofty, almost imperialistic way of imposing its message on us.

I've spoken about this with Sergio Zyman, Coca-Cola's chief marketing officer. He goes one step further. When commercials are tested, viewers inevitably like some and hate others. The simple fact that teenagers the world over have their favorite and least favorite Coke ads is, in Sergio Zyman's eyes, an achievement. He sees this as a sort of discussion topic for kids: "I like the "Polar Bear" and "Heartland" ads, but I don't like "Hypnosis" and the "Lyric Logo." Being able to like or dislike an ad brings the brand closer to you. The brand is less imposing. It is merely there, present, an unavoidable part of everyday life. It simply no longer wants to be perfect.

Defamiliarize

"It will reframe the familiar scene", adds Handy, "and it will reconceptualize the obvious." This idea of viewing the familiar in a different manner is critical. When campaigns resist change on the pretext of preserving continuity, when we see the same images year after year, we eventually fail even to notice them. They become as insignificant as they are familiar. In an article in *Marketing Insights*, Martin Landey extols the benefits of defamiliarization, using the magazine *Rolling Stone* as an example: "If advertising can't force you to rediscover products as if you've never seen them before, then you don't notice advertising." Advertising must reclaim its role of making the unstrange strange, the familiar unfamiliar.

Rolling Stone magazine is indeed a good example. As long as it was perceived as a posthippie publication, its advertising sales plummeted. Thanks to the Perception and Reality campaign, Fallon McElligott breathed new life into the magazine. Today, the image of this magazine from the 1960s has radically shifted. The familiar has been reframed. Overall circulation to consumers, as well as total ad page sales, have gone up.

For business people around the world, Dun & Bradstreet specializes in information concerning corporate viability. Period. Nobody thinks Dun & Bradstreet does anything else. And yet their knowledge of corporations, especially over the long term, is without equal. Hence the theme of its campaign: "We see what others don't" is an effective way of reframing the company's raison d'être. It elevates Dun & Bradstreet to the status of business consultant.

In France, Rodier was "defamiliarized." From a ready-to-wear line so classic it had become conservative, it was transformed into a contemporary brand. So contemporary, in fact, that the ads didn't hesitate to have women show their emotional and ultrafeminine sides. Rodier suddenly became the brand for women who feel good about themselves, women who lead active lives while remaining feminine. The result of this campaign's five-year run was a drop in the average age of the Rodier consumers by four years. When women wear Rodier, they not only see the brand differently, they see themselves differently as well.

Bartle Bogle Hegarty deserves unlimited praise for its work on Levi's in Europe. The strategy was all but banal; Levi's has been selling the United States and everything it incarnates to Europe for 30 years. What is new, however, is the way in which the product's history is revisited.

One commercial, shot in black and white, begins with a scene that is filmed from the perspective of a driver going down a bumpy dirt road in the middle of nowhere. The music intensifies as all we see are the legs of the mystery driver clad in Levi's getting out of the car. We follow the driver into an old-fashioned general store where we see the very puritanical-looking owner serving a mother and her young son. The merchant turns to the new customer while the camera focuses on the woman looking over the newcomer with a disapproving air. Both the woman and the store owner are aghast as we see a hand reach out to take a small tin of condoms and slide it into a pocket. We have yet to see the customer's face. We follow the mystery customer back into the car and drive to a Victorian-style house with an ominous facade. The driver runs up the stairs and rings the doorbell. The door opens. It is no other than the stern-faced store owner. When we expect a young girl to run down the stairs, the commercial takes an unexpected twist. Instead it is a good-looking young man who bounds down the stairs to meet his date. The mystery driver clad in Levi's is none other than the condom purchaser who turns out to be a beautiful young girl. As the young man bolts out the front door before his father can say a word, the camera freezes on his father's shocked expression next to which appear the words, "Watch pocket. Created in 1873. Abused ever since."

Never has a commercial so brilliantly married the authentic with the contemporary. The other films in this campaign all take a similar approach. In one, we learn that belt loops were added to jeans to facilitate tackling in the newly popular sport, American football. In another, we are told that Levi's got rid of its metal crotch rivets due to their inconvenient tendency to generate heat. And in another, we're shown the pain that people go through to keep their Levi's intact, given their short supply in wartime. By reinventing the product in a whimsical fashion, BBH defamiliarized it, giving it the touch of humor that wins us over every time. Faced with this level of creativity, people have no choice but to happily give in. They are disarmed.

Recomplexify

Reframe. Defamiliarize. Recomplexify, too. What a mouthful. Nonetheless, it's a way of saying that getting yourself to be perceived in a different way sometimes means refusing to accept simplification. Simplification can be insulting and harmful.

At Michelin headquarters in Clermont-Ferrand, France, 300 chemists and 500 physicists conduct research. It may come as a surprise, but in theory at least, a tire is nearly as complicated to design as an airplane. Whereas a plane flies through the air, tires are subjected to a multitude of contradictory forces applied by the road and the moving car. Whether people realize it—and most don't—a tire is a high-tech product. And while many people are convinced that the Michelin tire is superior, not many know how superior. Michelin is unsurpassed in its field. It does more than promise durability and performance; it goes a step further and guarantees both at once: long-lasting performance. This combination is the most technically difficult feat for a tire. As a result, advertising's sole option is to take a didactic approach. It must explain. The difference between a Michelin and a competitor's tire must be made greater. To illustrate the margin of superiority, the advertisement must reinforce the idea of technical difficulty in the mind of the viewer. In other words, it must recomplexify.

Michelin's need to recomplexify is shared by numerous other categories, especially low-interest ones. Whether it's household appliances or water and electric distribution, the public believes all products are equal and that things work just fine on their own. We recommended that the French leader of household appliances educate people that the technology for such products is sophisticated—for example, by explaining the wear and tear caused by opening a refrigerator door 120 times a day. We did the same for the Public Water Works and the National Electric Council. Now, the French no longer take for granted the water that flows from their taps or the electricity that illuminates their homes.

I would not go so far as to say that advertising (like mathematics and the social sciences) should revel in complexity, that quality so dear to American scientists and French philosophers. Too often, however, advertising is reductive. We must refuse to accept simplification and the "banalization" that ensues. In certain product categories we need to complexify. For advertising people accustomed to simplifying, that's a rather disruptive thought.

Why Disruption?

We've already noted that disruption is not the most elegant of words. What's worse is that the meaning we give the word is sometimes misunderstood. For some, when they are first introduced to Disruption, it seems to imply a systematic desire to shake up, overturn, cause chaos, upset. To eradicate everything. To these people, our response is that Disruption does not disrupt brands, it disrupts conventions. And the consequence is that we disrupt the marketplace to benefit our clients' brands. Nothing more, nothing less.

Disruption Anticipates

As we've seen, there are levels of disruption, a point that Batey, our partner in the Far East, also underlines. This distinction builds on Igor Ansoff's differentiated levels of turbulence, each of which requires a different response. Igor Ansoff emphasized that a growing level of turbulence signals a time not to react but to anticipate, not to solve a problem but to seize an opportunity. Creating a new level of turbulence yourself. In other words, to upset the balance of your market by doing things very differently. That's what Compaq did when it inverted its pricing policy to give clones a dose of their own medicine and why it's now way ahead of its competition. Or Southwest when it focused on regional routes and decided not to be all things to all people. Or Netscape when it made free software available, hoping that its popularity would spread by word of mouth.

Disruption must adapt to the state of the market, its turbulence level, as well as the maturity of the brand. This implies that you need to assess the extent of disruption needed by a given brand in a given market at a given time and to anticipate the degree of turbulence that can be introduced to a given market. Whether you create a low-degree turbulence like Clairol and BMW, or a high-degree one as in the case of TAG Heuer and Virgin, the most important thing is to anticipate. Disruption encourages it.

Disruption Builds Brands

A brand is an asset. More and more companies are including this intangible on their balance sheets. But as Larry Light, director of the Coalition for Brand Equity, points out, it's not so much the brand as the relationship between the brand and the customers that matters. "Brand loyalty is the asset," he says. You may then wonder how in the world we can suggest creating discontinuities when nothing is more important than the continuity of brand loyalty? It seems paradoxical at the least.

But only on the surface. Because everything moves, a brand cannot remain immobile. A brand is always in transition. It needs to evolve. It cannot remain stuck. It builds and reinforces itself day after day.

If a brand rests on its heritage, fails to question itself, and builds only on its past, before long it will come to appear complacent or static. It needs to be nourished with ideas and new initiatives. People need to sense that it is attentive to the times and that it knows how to remain contemporary. In fact, there is no paradox, no contradiction between Disruption and increasing brand loyalty. If companies and brands do not disrupt, there is an increased risk that consumers will become blasé and lose interest in brands. With Disruption, their interest and loyalty is renewed.

This is the end result of Disruption. It leads people to think about a brand in a new way, to freshen their idea of it. Disruption gives a lick of the whip, a spark of youth to the brands that are so dear to them. It puts them back in the spotlight. It is great to see their renewed vitality, their dynamism. If consumers like them already, they like them even more. They become enthusiasts. They feel even more loyal.

Some brands give the impression of truly believing in what they do. In the United States, examples of this include Southwest, Toys "Я" Us, and Ben & Jerry's. Their enthusiasm is contagious. They draw loyal customers in their wake. The same holds true for Snapple and MCI. Snapple has based all its advertising on its relationship with its customers, and actually encourages them to write to Snapple with stories and suggestions. "The best stuff on earth" campaign strives to establish a word-of-mouth phenomenon among its buyers. MCI, with its inventive Gramercy Press ad series, gets even closer to its customers. It has succeeded where its competitors have failed: concretely showing everything that's likable about the latest technology. People are grateful to those who know how to be useful. These brands maintain a very close rapport with their customers. They've done this right from the beginning, and through some form of disruption. They offered their customers something new. That is why they have enjoyed unsurpassed success in the last 10 years.

In an article I wrote for a French business magazine, I tried to emphasize that the ultimate goal of advertising is to give brands more meaning, more substance, more heft. To bring home this idea of thickness, I chose a title in English, "Think Thick." French readers understood what I meant. They didn't know it was poor English.

I went on to say that a brand shouldn't stop at being a name for a product people buy. Rather, it should be a point of reference, carrying with it an added psychological value, a value that makes the consumer say to himself, "Deep down, I'm happy I bought this." Therefore, the product must be given more meaning and perspective through the work done on the brand. Apple helps me fulfill my dreams, Oil of Olay relieves my anxiety, Nike pushes me to give it my all, Levi's for women celebrates womanhood, Keds brings me back to my childhood, and Pepsi makes me a part of new generations. All these names have a certain density or thickness. They are icons. Advertising has endowed them with spirit and *élan*, and secured them a place in the social context. They have perspective, and therefore have gone beyond the limits of the marketplace. Their competitors, by contrast, lack this meaning and depth.

Disruption Travels

Disruption is also an international asset. Disruption travels. TAG Heuer is a global campaign; Danone and Virgin are on the verge of being international campaigns. Insofar as they strengthen their brands, disruptions can be transferred from one country to another. IKEA, Häagen-Dazs, and Snapple are all easy to export. Even Saturn, despite the fact that it sells the spirit of the United States to Americans.

At a given moment in their brand life, Levi's, Apple, Nike, Pepsi, and Benetton (and even Coke in recent years) decided to cause a disruption. Each disruption has been an act of construction, of strengthening the idea of the brand. It reinforces the way consumers think of it. "Brands are ideas that people store away in their heads and in their hearts," the people at Young & Rubicam used to say. By being highly intrusive, these brands gained a long-lasting place in the mind of the world consumer. That's how they have gone global and are now unavoidable, ineradicable.

A final example is an old brand that not only manages to refresh itself, but travels: Danone. Five years ago, we advised Danone, the leader in fresh dairy products, to launch a major campaign based on health. Danone's spots are radically new in that they are quasi-institutional. In one of them, we see a boy, his father, his grandfather, and also his great-grandfather. The voice-over tells us, "Today people can expect to live 20 years longer than a century ago. Improved nutrition has helped make the difference. Tomorrow, thanks to research, our diet will be our primary defence. We'll have a better chance of being around to see how the latest arrival resembles his great-grandfather." An explanation of the Danone Institute for Health follows as well as a description of Danone's ever-growing investment in research. All of this boils down to, in French, *Entreprendre*

pour la santé. Loosely translated, it becomes, "Danone. Taking responsibility for your health."

Illustrating longer life expectancy by showing a child who's lucky enough to know his great-grandfather is a beautiful idea. It's also a way for Danone to appear warm and close. The brand shows it cares about the destiny of its customers. The Institute now exists in six countries. Tomorrow it will travel to many more. Each year in France, a study is conducted to determine the public's favorite brands, all categories combined. Five years ago, Danone ranked high, coming in fourth. The last few steps are always the hardest to climb. Today Danone is number one.

A Tool for Change

The time has passed when business people could sit back and quietly manage their assets. Their hold can be challenged at any time by anyone. Gone is the glorious pioneer era when brands were faced with a vast wilderness waiting to be conquered and settled. Forgotten are the days when a leader could momentarily let down his or her guard without suffering serious damage. Today, companies are constantly seeking out new territories in which to expand. Dozing off, even for a second, can be penalizing. Often irreversibly. More than ever, offense is the best defense. Our clients are no longer in a mind-set of continuous improvement, where strategies aim at doing a bit more or a bit better than the competition. Being better is not enough.

This is where we must prove our creativity and understand that creativity makes change possible. Creativity helps manage change.

Too often, advertising is limited to reinforcing the status quo, to confirming what the brand has always been. The vocabulary used is anchored in the past: Agencies talk of a brand's capital, its stock, its foundations, its genetic makeup. We constantly return to a brand's roots, to its heritage. And we forget that advertising can also be a tool for a change. It can propose a vision that propels the brand forward. A vision that accelerates. It can be the sign, the proof that an even brighter future awaits the brand.

That is why the goal of Disruption is to help companies and their brands to make leaps—not just creative leaps, but strategic ones as well.

77

Disruption

Disruption signifies at once a break with the past, a leap in relation to the present, and a step toward the future. More than a philosophy, it is an actual practice. A state of mind. A discipline that creates disorder and stimulates change. As the saying goes, "If you don't create change, change will create you."

5

CONVENTION

IN 1968, VALERI BRUMEL still held the world's record for high jumping. He was the first to clear 2.20 meters, which at the time seemed tremendously high. He had a clean, pure style. There was a supreme, near-perfect elegance in his movement. He was living proof that an unadorned style was the key to effectiveness.

Then came Dick Fosbury. Before him, everybody had tackled high jumping using the same technique: the Western roll. In Mexico, in 1968, Fosbury showed the world a revolutionary way of high jumping, one that no one before had ever considered using. Fosbury disrupted the one convention of high jumping, which was that the only way to go over the bar is on your front.

Dick Fosbury became an Olympic champion. And today, high jumpers use the Fosbury Flop and finish with their backs to the bar.

A disruption must have a starting point, a foundation. We must do everything to see what others are blind to. We can't create a rupture from nothing. Before Fosbury, it had never crossed anyone's mind that the high jump could be executed any other way than on your front.

Brumel was the convention, albeit execution at its apogee. Fosbury was the disruption, a figurative and tangible leap forward.

Conventions Are Departure Points

We have seen that Disruption is a three-step process. The first step consists in uncovering the convention that will serve as a catalyst. Departure from a convention gives birth to disruption.

Before elaborating on our interpretation of convention, let's revisit the dictionary definition: A *convention* is "an accepted rule, that which it is customary to think and do, that which is in keeping with established rules." In other words, conventions are all the things we accept without realizing it, such as habits and customs that become firmly implanted and that we no longer question. In other words, established behavior so familiar it's no longer noticeable.

Few have spoken about challenging the accepted truths as inspiringly as Sir Alan Sheppard, the chairman of Grand Metropolitan. He acknowledges that change is uncomfortable, that it creates friction and calls up uncertainties. He stresses that his method consists in "orchestrating anarchy, within a clear strategy" and believes that it is the only way to release the energy and the talent of employees, and to turn them into entrepreneurs. He expects them to look for radical new ways of doing things. To push back the perimeter of the possible. He uses the very evocative expression, "antigravitational management" and even goes as far as to use the tag line of the famous Heineken campaign to urge his company to seek change "that refreshes the parts that other cultures haven't yet reached."

Alan Sheppard illustrates what we all know intuitively: Habit breeds comfort, which in turn prevents change. Identifying the familiar is the first step in preparing for a leap. Moving toward a disruption. Conventions are departure points for creating intrusive strategies which in turn lead to unexpected executions.

Three Types of Conventions

Conventions are infinite; our beliefs are anchored by them. When it comes to communication and creating disruption, we are concerned with three broad types: marketing, consumer, and advertising conventions.

Convention

Marketing Conventions

Marketing conventions reveal what clients think of themselves, of their role, the target, the competition, and their offer. They are beliefs such as: Line extensions invariably dilute brand image; certain products are inherently low interest; computers are the domain of business specialists; in retail, the only way to move merchandise is by slashing prices . . . and so on. These are the kinds of conventions, ingrained ways of thinking, that influence any marketing plan.

Let's look at tires again. Everyone thinks that they're not interesting. In France, barely 20 percent of drivers know the brand of tire on their cars. If the product is uninteresting, it's probably futile to strive to come up with a superior product. And, it's irrelevant to then do product advertising: The public will just ignore it. Rather than getting lost in the details of the shape of the  tread or its coefficient of elasticity, one may infer that it would be more effective to produce flashy commercials that focus on the brand. And to forget about the product. Wrong. That's a convention—and the one Michelin overturned. Its commercials in Europe have a technological content and a rigorous tone. They even go so far as to squeeze mathematical equations onto television screens. Given their style, one might expect that these commercials would achieve inferior recall and likeability ratings to the category standard. The opposite occurred. Michelin's ratings have always been superior and offer proof that, contrary to popular belief, any product can be interesting.

In Europe, Michelin's competitors do brand advertising, totally unrelated to the product. That's conventional thinking. And Michelin has challenged it.

Consumer Conventions

Consumer conventions are most often preconceived ideas. Ideas that everyone shares. They can take the form of those expressions that, by virtue of being overused, become void of meaning, such as "the simpler, the better," or "seeing is believing," or "nothing is better than being there." Conventions can also be about a product category. Think, for example, about such common perceptions as: Inexpensive furniture means low quality or insurance companies only try to avoid reimbursements. Conventions can be even more profound when the consumption of such-and-such a product is inextricably linked to the perceptions people have of themselves when they buy that product. When people buy perfume, follow fashion, or choose a brand of liquor, it's hard for them to escape their preconceived notions. So many product categories, so many widespread opinions, so many conventions. Behaviors and beliefs make conventions infinite.

There are also those markets that seem to offer the same products. We sometimes get the impression that total commoditization is unavoidable. Think about the major rental car companies. The overall feeling is that they all offer the same services. Pretty much. But, only pretty much, as Hertz stresses. For three years, Hertz has been reminding us that "In rent-a-cars, there's Hertz and not exactly." Through the "not exactly" theme and the commitment it implies, Hertz refuses commoditization. Everything can't and shouldn't be reduced to a price war. Hertz fights the convention that you cannot differentiate the quality of service. Hertz reintroduces the idea of a difference. Its commercials suddenly make us doubt the quality of Hertz's competition. Are they really doing the same thing? Exactly?

Advertising Conventions

Advertising conventions deal with registers of expression and executional approaches. They are the conventions that influence the way advertisers do advertising. For example: Problem/solution is the most effective format for household products; car advertising must showcase the car; soft drink advertising is about selling lifestyles; shampoos, like any performance product, should focus on the end result; light beer advertising should reassure the consumer about its taste. . . .

More often than not, advertising is coded. Too much so. Each category generates its own mannerisms. You never see cosmetic advertising without a top model, a commercial for a food product without appetizing ingredients, a campaign for a holiday resort without the inevitable sun, or a cognac ad without the stereotypical symbols of style and refined taste.

Every product category creates its own rules, as advertising people do their own idiosyncrasies.

Advertising conventions are therefore those common approaches that result from habits or reflexes commonly used by advertising agencies to treat a given subject. For instance, because most of the time adults are the ones who buy pet food at the supermarket, pet food advertising is always targeted to them. That's a convention. In Holland, Quaker's dog food campaign targets children, for the simple reason that 50 percent of dogs' masters are children. Therefore, the strategy is built unconventionally on  the affection that exists between children and their pets. Very distinctive. The advertising target is neither the consumer nor the buyer.

A Convention Is an Opinion

It's not just the facts that influence, but rather the opinions and beliefs people have about facts. Apple, Absolut, Michelin, Snapple, and Clairol Herbal Essences are all examples of going against widespread opinions—in other words, confronting conventional thinking.

It's not always easy to separate facts from opinions. Often, a point of view is mistaken for an incontestable reality. The key is in telling the difference between the two. That's when the interpretation stage begins. Because everyone has access to the same information, it's clearly the way one interprets it that brings added value.

A Polaroid camera can capture emotions on the spot, and reproduce them in an instant. That is a fact. So people save their Polaroid for occasions such as birthdays and weddings, to capture all the fun of those memorable moments. They believe that a Polaroid is only for special events. That is an opinion. People forget that an instant camera can come in handy in a thousand other situations. In order to get consumers to take out their instant cameras more often, Polaroid came up with a campaign that details its everyday uses: The plumber taking a photo as proof of his work, a woman leaving on her husband's desk a picture of the antique she wants to buy . . . and so on. Polaroid becomes a sort of visual memo. At the end of each commercial, the claim appears on the screen in the form of a question: "What has Polaroid done for you today?" The question took Europeans

by surprise. They realized that they had a predetermined notion of the product. Americans had the same reaction to the recent "See what develops" campaign.

The consumer often has preconceived beliefs. The marketer does as well. For example, brand management follows preset rules such as: A brand should act as a small company within a company. This means that each brand has its own profitability, its own long- and short-term goals, and, therefore, its own advertising budget. As company head, the brand manager alone must determine the amount of money to invest in advertising for the brand. Had Danone rigidly applied this conventional allocation system, the "Taking responsibility for your health" umbrella campaign would never have seen the light of day. This transversal campaign is financed by all 30 or 40 Danone products. Each brand manager agreed to chip in a bit of his or her advertising budget toward the effort. Thus, the way funds were allocated has been modified. Standard procedures were shaken up.

No disruption is substantial or lasting unless it has breached a common way of acting or thinking. A widespread opinion that has turned into a convention. The trick is uncovering that convention. The moment you're exposed to the convention, you say "Why, of course, I just never thought about it that way. This is solid good sense." It's true that pulling out the Polaroid only once a year is a waste. After all, a Polaroid could be extremely useful. It's true that tires are not so boring. So much is riding on them. It's true that kids love their dogs. Quaker was the first to notice that no advertising was aimed at children. Each time, a way of doing something has been questioned. An opinion has been challenged.

What a Convention Isn't

When you're introduced to the idea of overturning a convention, you may simply think that it's a euphemism for doing something different. *Uncon-*

ventional. But, thinking in terms of conventions and striving to disrupt them goes way beyond that.

Because a convention is based on an insight, something that's hidden, departing from convention leads to doing much more than differentiating oneself. If something hidden isn't uncovered, there won't be a convention—thus, no disruption. We look to find a convention. Beforehand. And our job is to draw it out of hiding, to bring it to the surface. The Germans like to say, "Discovery is seeing what everybody has seen and thinking what nobody has thought."

One might also mistakenly think that overturning conventions simply means doing the opposite of what everyone else does. In other words, doing what is often referred to as *contrarian marketing.* By positioning itself as the Un-Cola, 7-Up fought against the tyranny of cola that young people's choice was limited to Coke or Pepsi. The cola monopoly was attacked head-on by 7-Up. While this is an example where contrarian marketing and overturning conventions overlap, these examples are rare.

It is usually not enough to say or do the opposite of what others do or say. That fallacy is a trap into which many fall. If you define yourself or your product by counterpoint alone, you risk appearing hollow, meaningless.

Pepsi, Nike, Virgin, Snapple, Polaroid, and Danone have all attacked conventions. But the disruptions they have caused in their respective markets have been less direct and often more clever than simple contradictions. You can oppose something without proposing its opposite. Like Nike and Danone, you must offer something else—a new vision of the market and of the brand's role within it.

Discovering Conventions

Identifying and challenging the right conventions requires a drastic departure from standard approaches to strategy development. It starts with breaking out of usual thinking patterns.

Unlearning

It is difficult to "leap out of the box." And even more so if you can't define the box you're in. You have to know what it is you're trying to escape from.

That is what working on conventions is all about. We live inside mental frames that limit our perceptions. We must learn how to break free.

> **"Did you ever try to forget something?"**
> **Tom Peters**

To discover a convention, which is most often hidden, you must unlearn. Try your best to free your mind of mental habits and of the sum of the things you know. "One lifetime," wrote the philosopher Henri Michaud, "is not enough to unlearn everything one has learned."

Unlearning is a discipline. It leads to questioning what has until present proved effective, and to benefiting from other people's experience and imagination. It's about approaching subjects differently and refusing to adopt thought patterns that reassure. Thinking in terms of Disruption helps to unlearn. It is a catalyst. While it has its own special logic and in the beginning requires a certain amount of effort to get used to, we all find in Disruption a way to question our own ways of thinking.

Commonalities

When you're trying to uncover a convention, you think about the most common reflexes, about the habits shared by the greatest number of people. You trace the commonalities, not the differences, among disparate groups of people.

In this respect, Disruption is an approach that contrasts with the way most agencies think. This is a crucial point. Agencies are accustomed to looking for divergent rather than convergent points. They draw maps, plot the brands on them, and try to distinguish them from each other. They wonder what the criteria of differentiation could be. Working on conventions does the opposite. It identifies what all the brands scattered across the maps have in common. If that common point exists, if there is something that is shared by all the brands, it will be the potential starting point of a disruption.

Conventions are not narrow. They unify people. They are not opinions shared by one group in particular. They unite people regardless of age, background, and habits. In any market there are visible disparities in the way a brand or a product is perceived. For example, brand users do not have the same feeling as nonusers. The former have very good reasons to buy the brand, while the latter, too, have very good reasons not to buy it. That being said, a convention embraces both users and nonusers alike. Although they don't share the same feelings about the brand, there are surely points of view these people do have in common. Identifying those perceptions will be a source of disruption.

When we conduct focus groups, we often include both users and nonusers in the same meeting. After listening to the disagreements for a long time, we search for the points on which the interviewees agree. This is always an enriching exercise. It is how we discovered that even European bleach nonusers believe that nothing beats bleach when it comes to disinfection. Or that French women always keep flour in the back of the cupboard, out of sight, out of mind. Or that many people add a second spoonful of instant coffee to their cup. Even those who don't do this believe that others do.

Each time we discover a universal attitude or behavior, something that embraces the greatest number of people, and we capitalize on it before the competition does, we find the seed of a disruptive campaign. Conventions are not exclusive. They are inclusive.

Challenging Conventions

Our habits are so deeply anchored that they often seem impossible to change. They are carved in stone. Through our own inattentiveness, some things have become too familiar. Then, suddenly, what was once hidden from view is laid bare. All because we questioned the givens and threw off the yoke of habitual patterns of thought. We simply asked ourselves, "Why? Why is it like this?" Which invariably leads to the question, "Why can't it be different?"

Convention meetings kick off the investigational phase, the goal of which is to "see" more clearly. The moment in which we return to the facts and ask ourselves, *Why don't adults drink milk? Why is it more desirable for a pair of jeans to look American? Why is cereal a breakfast food? Why do American cars try to look and act Japanese? Why do people drink orange juice in the morning? Why does beer advertising always celebrate masculinity and scenes of male bonding?* Flushing conventions out of their hiding place takes time. You have to delve deeply into them with your eyes wide open. By asking questions again and again, you end up exposing one or even several conventions. Then you have to choose the one that is the most inspiring, the most promising.

Let's look at beer advertising in Great Britain, which is among the most brilliant in the world. Nevertheless, it had its conventions, too. Both agencies and marketers believed the ad should take place in a pub and be funny. We should note that 70 percent of all Brits cite going to the pub as their primary leisure activity. That is a fact. Only 20 percent of the beer consumed in Great Britain is drunk at home. "Sociability, conviviality, and masculinity" are the key words here. This fact translates into the convention that any decent beer advertisement must portray groups of men relaxing over a pint of beer in a pub. Such an opinion was widely held, until Heineken came along and demonstrated that you can succeed without any of that. With the "It refreshes the parts other beers can't reach" campaign, Heineken was the first beer that escaped from the entrenched stereotypes surrounding beer.

Recent beer advertising in the United Kingdom has followed the Heineken example. Going against the grain has become the convention. Castlemaine XXXX, an imported Australian beer, bucked the notion that a beer must seem and act like a native product. Instead, Castlemaine extolled its heritage and positioned itself as the renegade beer. In the ale segment, Murphy's humanizes a product attribute and becomes the beer for people who, like Murphy's, "aren't bitter." As for John Smith Bitter, it's a case in itself. All draft-in-a-can beers typically celebrate their taste and frothiness. They position themselves as the creamy draft beers that you can drink at home. John Smith's, as a late entrant to a crowded niche, decided to own the cause of the creaminess, not the effect. It challenged the convention that one should never do category advertising. In other

words, John Smith's dared to claim the one reason-why that differentiates the entire category, the in-can device. It preempted the generic category attribute in an intelligent fashion and became the market leader.

By asking the right questions and identifying and overturning the most fertile conventions, a leap occurs . . . one reminiscent of Fosbury. The California Milk Board got adults to realize that milk was the best companion beverage for their favorite foods, Polaroid proved that instant photography is a tool for everyday life, Kellogg's cornflakes got the British to see cereal as an anytime snack, Saturn acted uncompromisingly American, and, as we've seen, beer advertisers in the United Kingdom understood that to be heard and seen in such a crowded market, one has to disrupt.

Not Overturning a Raison-d'Être

When we explain them after the fact, all these conventions might appear obvious. Apparent. But just because a convention leads to a very disruptive idea doesn't mean that it's the one you should challenge. Take Bic, for example, who has made several attempts at launching its own perfume, with nononsense packaging and a low price tag. That strategy focused on trying to convince the consumer that the only thing that really matters is the perfume inside the bottle. These attempts have been overwhelmingly unsuccessful because the market convention that perfume evokes luxury is so deeply entrenched. Luxury is even more than a convention. It's the category's raison d'être. In this case, Bic's approach was iconoclastic.

There are things that are fixed, and those that are flexible. The key to working through conventions is obviously to distinguish between the two.

When Vision Precedes Convention

Logic would dictate tackling the three steps of the Disruption process in order: Study the conventions, uncover the preconceived notions, create a rupture, which in turn gives birth to an enduring brand image. However, as I have already stressed, Disruption is a nonlinear process, which encourages entering the process at any of its three stages.

Preexisting Visions

A company can have a preexisting vision. This was true for Virgin, Snapple, and Nike. Oddly enough in this case, when we work on the disruption format, the vision is written first and then we move back upstream to determine the most germane convention. So how do you link the two? Simply by identifying the conventions that are an obstacle to the brand vision. Standard retail logic would have run counter to Virgin's vision, which deals with the intangible and the cultural. Michelin has a very technology-oriented vision. The convention here says that people are not interested in tires and that it's hopeless to try to get them interested. This is an obstacle to the vision. Polaroid wants to position itself as a useful, everyday object. It must therefore fight against its own image of being reserved exclusively for special occasions such as weddings and birthdays.

If you manage to identify the convention that clashes most with the vision, you can turn it into the starting point of your advertising. The route leading to the vision will be that much shorter.

Until recently, Liberty Mutual had been branded as just another insurance company, stiff and insensitive, like its counterparts. But Liberty Mutual's behavior was anything but that. There was an unexploited opportunity to share its unusual programs with the public that together demonstrated an unspoken vision that insurance is about problem prevention.

Each commercial documents one way that Liberty is helping people to live safer, more secure lives and offers tangible proof that an insurance company should be a problem preventer. Problem preventer is the vision. Problem solver, the convention.

There is another company that has a radical vision about the way its market should be and act. Oddbins is a British wine store that believes that buying wine should be as much fun as drinking it. A vision that is completely at odds with its stuffy competition that approaches wine as a fine art.

Oddbins celebrated its informality and anti-establishment personality across the board: Its salespeople, its store set-up, and its advertising. By doing so, it overturned the entrenched market convention and gave birth to a new vision for its market. A vision that it alone owns.

When the Product Is Disruptive

Sometimes the work is already done for you: The product itself goes against the grain. Apple, IKEA, and Saturn, by their very nature, defied predetermined ideas. Unlike Bic, they overturned conventions that were questionable. When this is the case, advertising people should limit their role to being mere interpreters. The advertising is the reflection of the product's stance. Apple waged a frontal attack on IBM; its advertising portrayed Big Brother. IKEA questions the validity of intermediary costs; its commercials show us caricatures of salespeople. Saturn challenges the superiority of Japanese cars; its commercials relaunch the power of "Made in America." It took Japanese cars 10 years to become a "must." It took Saturn less than 12 months to demolish the preconceived notion that Japanese equaled better.

In each of these examples—Apple, IKEA, Saturn—the product itself is a discontinuity. If the advertising deliberately sticks to illustrating that discontinuity, it is naturally disruptive.

The Discipline of Doubt

A successful company, if it wants to continue to prosper, is obliged to question itself, to discover its own conventions. To do so, it has to bring together the sum of its experiences with those of the outside world. This is one of the missions of Disruption.

Any company's intellectual capital deteriorates. To invent a future for yourself, you have to free yourself from the past. If you settle for merely solidifying what you've already got, you end up stuck in a mental rut. You idle. You doze. You lose the tendency to constantly question. Paul Valéry, the poet and philosopher, recommended waking up from a thought that has lasted too long.

If it is true that success comes to those who dare rethink the rules of the game, our goal is that Disruption change the rules of the advertising game.

It is imperative that agencies find the freshness they have too often lost, locked as they are in a market logic that they no longer challenge, and that they resist the waves of dominant thought.

"A certitude is nothing other than a lack of imagination," Descartes told us. So long as we have not doubted, we cannot claim to have thought.

Doubt must be cultivated like a discipline. In the Disruption process, the convention stage is the time for questioning. It is the "why" step. When you ask why, you end up one day wondering "why not?" That is when you get a glimpse of your brand's share of the future. That is how visions are created.

6

VISION

"I WILL BUILD a motor car for the great multitude. It will be constructed of the best materials, by the best men and women to be hired, after the simplest designs that modern engineering can devise. Any person making a good salary will be able to own one. And enjoy with his family the blessings of hours of pleasure. In God's great open spaces."

The Ford Motor Company is still living by these words today. Henry Ford was a visionary.

Time has passed. Because of the word *vision*'s overuse, employed in any and all situations, it has lost some of its meaning. *The Economist* published an article entitled "The Vision Thing," which illustrated how fuzzy the meaning has become. The term is all used up. It seems as if vision has become a fad.

But despite its overuse, I believe that vision in its truest sense remains pertinent. As companies move ahead more and more rapidly, diversify at breakneck speeds, go through the necessary reengineering stages, and become more and more decentralized, they need something to keep them cohesive and strong. Vision lends direction to all this movement. A vision is a shaping force.

Ford sought to democratize the automobile; Apple, to free people from the tyranny of computers; Boeing, to bring air travel to the masses; Nike, to make each one of us an accomplished sportsperson; CNN, to provide nonstop global news for worldwide audiences. Honda makes the way in which its engineers see cars its guiding light. In other words, Honda does not build cars that customers dream of, but ones that manufacturers do. Nordstrom elevates shopping to a pleasant experience. It is not a specialty clothing retailer, but a "provider of a lifetime, user-friendly relationship only marginally associated with clothing per se."

The founder of The Body Shop has a distinctive viewpoint: That cosmetics are overpackaged, overpriced, and overadvertised. Her vision "to make compassion, care, harmony, and trust the foundation stones of business" reflects beliefs very different from her competition. Quite disruptive.

Without these guiding lights, although perhaps not expressed in terms of a "vision," these companies would not have achieved such considerable market successes. Nothing is more powerful and motivating for companies than identifying with something they stand for and aspire to. What we refer to as a vision. It goes beyond a simple reason for being, a guiding philosophy, or a sense of purpose. It drives every initiative that the brand undertakes.

Vision Revisited

Now, more than ever, companies need visions in their truest sense. They need to step back, to regain perspective, and to imagine what share of the future will be theirs. It's at this point, that agencies have a role to play. Because they are so intimate with brands, they can help companies create and solidify visions.

Part Dream

The future can be imagined, not predicted. The same goes for vision. Neither market nor consumer research is capable of determining what a brand's vision ought to be. They can only assess a hypothesis' validity once it has been put forth. If you extrapolate the future from the present, you are thinking only with the rational, left side of the brain. By contrast, starting with a vision is like "thinking from right to left."

Clearly, a vision must be justified, supported by an analysis of trends, demographics, lifestyles, new regulations, and technological discontinuities. It must have a solid foundation. But it needs more than that. It must be compelling. Galvanizing. It must make people audacious, so that they outdo themselves. Visions are made of dreams.

It is possible to imagine great futures and be pragmatic at the same time. To come up with great visions and be action-oriented. Setting goals without an element of dream is a sterile exercise. Martin Luther King Jr. and John F. Kennedy showed us the way. George Bernard Shaw's "Some men see things as they are and ask why. I dream things that never were and ask why not" became Robert Kennedy's anthem for change.

Inspirational and Aspirational

A vision is really an idealized image of one's company. It's about striving toward an ideal. It is something that the entire company must stretch itself to achieve. It's a kind of goal that will never be reached. It's like a never-ending hurdle race. There is no finish line, no time limit.

For us, a vision is more than just a mission, more than a mere positioning. A great vision is the perfect fusion of what a company, product, or service is capable of standing for over time and what the end user really needs. It is a leap from where it is now to a larger, more ambitious scale.

A good vision is both aspirational and inspirational. It is something that, for the time being, is not within reach, although it is highly desirable. It draws people to it. In this sense, a vision is aspirational. The vision also inspires everything the brand does. Advertising then takes on a new role, that of reflecting the brand's vision in whatever it creates.

A vision draws the brand's initiatives upward. It can lead to a disruption, which in turn gives it its power. Everything converges. Think of the Apple launch commercial. Steve Jobs' vision that computers should be at the service of mankind, and not the reverse, was aspirational. Without it, Lee Clow would never have been inspired to use Orwell's *1984* "And you will see why 1984 won't be like 1984" for Macintosh. That sentence made people understand Apple's vision in an instant, and in a single airing on television.

That is disruption's principle advantage. It accelerates the journey to the vision.

Brand and Company Vision

Johnson & Johnson believes: "Our first responsibility is to the doctors, nurses, and patients, the mothers and all the others who use our products, who use our services. In meeting their needs, everything we do must be of high quality. We must constantly strive to reduce our costs in order to maintain reasonable prices. Customer orders must be serviced promptly and accurately. Our suppliers and distributors must have an opportunity to make a fair profit."

This credo is what Johnson & Johnson refers to as a vision. A corporate vision. Translated at the brand level, however, the vision for its baby powder takes on a new form, a different focus: "For more than fifty years, Johnson's Baby Powder has been consistently personified as the instrument of communicating a mother's love to her baby. No other baby product even comes close to Johnson's Baby Powder as a pure, unadulterated symbol of a mother's love." For me, this is what a vision should be. Highly inspirational. After decades of seeing the campaigns, all mothers know what Johnson & Johnson baby products stand for.

A corporate vision and a brand vision are not the same thing. You can see the difference between the two. The same word designates modes of thought that only partially overlap.

In annual reports, expressions of corporate visions often revolve around market domination, customer orientation, and company reorganization. They sound like mission statements. That's their role. You would not speak of mother's love in a company mission statement. Brand vision statements are more human and more consumer-oriented: They talk to each one of us. They serve a completely different purpose. They are at once a beacon and a source of inspiration for the brand.

Getting to Vision

A vision is not a set of objectives. Creating a vision is not about gathering facts. Rather, it's about using your imagination with a precise target in mind. If a vision is to be inspirational, it must reflect a deep understanding of the brand and project it into the future.

Understanding the Brand

People who are the most intimate with brands are those who come up with apt and meaningful visions. For Phil Knight, Nike is and will remain "the sweaty side of health and fitness, together with the romance of it." When asked to comment on one of his rare failures, his foray into casual shoes, Knight simply said, "Understanding the consumer is just one part of good marketing. You also have to understand the brand." Clearly he realized, after the fact, that casual shoes had no place in his brand definition.

"IBM used to mean a company, a way of doing business, a guaranteed solution to a business problem, security for the customer. When they changed all that, and made IBM mean just machines, they radically altered the value of that brand," Max Blockston wrote not long ago. In the last two years, IBM has experienced one of the most spectacular recoveries in the history of American business. Every aspect of the company has been reassessed. A lot has changed, and this transformation obviously had to be reflected in IBM's advertising. IBM now presents itself as the provider of "solutions for a small planet." IBM is recentering itself precisely on what made it successful, as a company that guarantees solutions. IBM has refocused itself on its original vision.

A vision must be at once ambitious and legitimate. To help create a fertile one, an advertising person must live with the brand, feel it, and know it like the back of his hand. Nike and IBM are examples of how understanding a brand led to a relevant vision. So are Pepsi and Danone.

Several 10-year-old kids, sitting on a hill, are watching the preparations for Woodstock II. Sipping a Pepsi, one says to the other, "This is the anniversary of a historic event." Another asks, "Which one?" The first boy answers, "Watergate." Thanks to BBDO, Pepsi is a brand in great shape. Whether it's this commercial or one that speaks directly to today's teenagers by using Michael Jackson, MC Hammer, or Cindy Crawford, all of them combine humor and dazzle with panache. For the last 20 years,

Phil Dusenberry has lent energy and wit to Pepsi. On the agency side, no one knows the brand better than he does.

I, too, am lucky enough to have worked for 20 years for the same brand:

Danone, a brand that stands for both health and pleasure worldwide. Yet the scale was never balanced between the two, nor was there uniform emphasis on one side or the other the world over. Take, for instance, the differences between Danone in France and Dannon in the United States.

In the United States, Dannon's brand image has always been health oriented. Its diet-consciousness results from campaigns such as "Get a Dannon Body." By contrast, in France, Danone's health image lacked substance. It needed to be reinforced. To drive Danone's new focus on health, our recent "Active Health" campaign includes commercials on taste education, immune defenses, and life expectancy, and soon to come, a commercial on diet and nutrition for senior citizens. The campaign demonstrates that what we eat is our primary medicine and that Danone teaches us something about our health every day.

Yet not all of Danone's products in France do or should subscribe to a "healthy" discourse. The brand also markets desserts. Indeed, it has just launched a triple-layered delight (vanilla, caramel, and whipped cream). It's hard to imagine anything more indulgent. This, however, in no way contradicts the overall image the brand conveys. Although Danone makes yogurt, which translates as health, and desserts, which obviously do not, all its products are fresh. It is there that health and pleasure overlap. Thus, the more the yogurt embodies health, the more the desserts benefit, and Danone can permit itself to launch products at the other end of the spectrum.

In the United States, Dannon has also recently found a happy medium between health and pleasure. It went in the opposite direction of its French counterpart and emphasized the indulgent side of its products. Although Danone's worldwide brand image tends to give more weight to health than to pleasure, it must not become an exclusively "healthy" brand: At the end of the day, it has to taste good. That is the truth of the Danone brand. One of Dannon's claims in the United States, "How can something that is so good for you taste so good?," put it perfectly.

Having a vision is the opposite of wearing blinders. A brand can rarely be reduced to a single element. Usually it comprises a multitude of different dimensions. The fact that one of them predominates in the vision in no way means that the others are unimportant. Unfortunately, people in advertising produce single-minded messages. They are accustomed to reducing everything to one dimension. They are too often ad led and too rarely brand led.

Great Visions Are Unique

The Body Shop, Toys "Я" Us, Saturn, and The Gap have visions of their very own. They are excellent examples of what Al Ries and Jack Trout call "the law of dominance." This law states that it's more valuable to be first than to be better. The purpose of marketing is to "envision a category, a field of reference in which you can be first." If in a given market you're not in first place, it's up to you to create a category within that market in which you will be number one.

A great vision will reflect this. Or rather, support it. It will enable the brand to be perceived differently from similar brands. It will help create the category. The Gap is a category unto itself. Saturn isn't far from being one, and Danone, too, is on its way.

The corollary to this law of being first is what Ries and Trout call "the law of focus." They explain the necessity of owning a word, the way Federal Express *owns* overnight, Volvo *owns* safety, Crest *owns* cavities, and Lysol *owns* disinfection. The law of focus is a bit simplistic. There are not a lot of words that can be owned, but the underlying principle still applies: You have to own something. That's the only way for a vision to be effective and stand the test of time. You have to own an idea. "Just do it" is an idea that embodies Nike's vision. "A lifetime of beautiful skin" is another that expresses the vision of Oil of Olay. "Taking responsibility for your health" sums up the vision of Danone.

Inspiration Sources

Searching for a vision isn't easy. And with good reason: You don't know what you're looking for. One good way to make progress is to ask yourself, "What should I base the vision on?" There are many sources, many open doors.

Inspiration sources can be found at three levels: The product, the brand, and the company itself. We have found that strong and fruitful visions often spring up as follows: at the *product* level, redefining product performance or looking at a category in a new light; at the *brand* level, basing oneself on the brand's expertise or giving that expertise new meaning; and at the *company* level, highlighting a company's savoir faire or emphasizing its role.

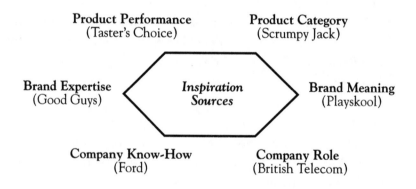

Product Performance
(Taster's Choice)

Product Category
(Scrumpy Jack)

Brand Expertise
(Good Guys)

*Inspiration
Sources*

Brand Meaning
(Playskool)

Company Know-How
(Ford)

Company Role
(British Telecom)

It's not an easy task for an instant coffee to claim superiority over real coffee. Yet that's what Taster's Choice has managed to do in the United States. Its commercials take the form of a serial soap opera that traces the budding love story between neighbors. The story begins when he borrows her Taster's Choice. Through their romance, Taster's Choice demonstrates that instant coffee is not a simple imitation of the real thing and that the coffee experience is about enhancing human relationships and bringing warmth to our lives. This avoids the instant coffee issue altogether and becomes the proof that *product performance* does not merely stop at taste.

In the United Kingdom, the cider category suffered from an inferiority complex vis-à-vis beer. Cider ads were a poor imitation of beer commercials. Thanks to Scrumpy Jack, the category has experienced a turnaround. A change of heart. Cider is no longer ashamed of being cider. Instead, the advertising personifies Scrumpy Jack as being so proud of his rare cider apples that he becomes obsessive about protecting them. Scrumpy Jack, by playing proudly on cider's heritage, threw new light on the *product category*.

You need a healthy dose of audacity to call your company The Good Guys! It's a promise you have to keep every day. The people who work for this California retailer specializing in television and stereo equipment do keep theirs. They have their own vision of service. For them, better service means total service. That's their *brand expertise*. Its advertising is testimony that its customers can ask The Good Guys! anything.

Playskool sees the child not as a being who is destined to grow up but as a personality that needs encouragement to blossom. The company does not consider itself a mere toy manufacturer, but rather an agent in a child's development. From a discovery mat that introduces infants to sensations and colors to a four-in-one activity center that encourages kids to paint, file, write, and build, Playskool has toys to encourage each stage of a child's growth. Being the child's educator is Playskool's *brand meaning*.

The birth of an automobile is always a big event. Engineers, supervisors, and workers labor for years until the day when the new model is finally ready. Car manufacturers usually call the first vehicle to come off the assembly line "Job 1." Fifteen years ago, Ford implemented a sweeping quality program that it has applied to model after model. The results are there. The new concentration on this *company know-how* has yielded its fruits. In 1994, Ford produced the highest number of defect-free cars among domestic producers and narrowed the quality gap with its Japanese competitors to 8 percent. This is obviously an exceptional achievement. On the advertising side, Ford's "Quality is Job 1" has become a very popular claim. Last year, in a consumer test that tracked print campaign recognition, Ford's "Quality is Job 1" tested first, ahead of Lexus, Absolut Vodka, Reebok, Calvin Klein, and even Marlboro.

The final domain is *company role*. British Telecom's advertising illustrates how a company can give itself a role. Its most celebrated commercial features Stephen Hawking, who despite being paraplegic has gone beyond his physical limitations to become one of the most reknowned physicists and writers on modern technology. When a man who can't speak without the help of a mechanical voice box actually is given a voice that tells us that communication is the only way to ensure progress, we listen. When we hear Stephen Hawking's simulated voice narrate the powerful images of deserts being turned into palaces of technology that float across the screen and tell us that "mankind's greatest achievements have come about by talking and its greatest failures by not talking," we're taken in and understand the profound content of his message. He continues "Our greatest hopes can become reality in the future with the help of modern technology. All we need to do is make sure we keep talking." This commercial reveals that BT doesn't content itself with selling small product improvements here and new product offerings there. Instead, British Telecom has decided to act as the advocate, not merely the agent, of communication. By taking on a role, it is transforming itself from a faceless bureaucratic enterprise to a human one, implicated in the lives of the people it serves.

Viewpoint: An Alternative to Vision

For some people, and in particular for those who work in the field of fast-moving consumer goods, vision is too grand a word. They say a firm can be visionary, but question a brand's capacity to be so. They ask "What about a brand of packaged goods? What about a Jell-O or a Palmolive?"

I believe that whether it's a company or a brand, vision thinking helps us to see the big picture—for example, active health for Danone Dairy Products or taste education for Amora Condiments. Both Danone and Amora are packaged goods. And both stand for something great.

Yet, to distinguish between visions for companies and for brands, I sometimes propose another term: *viewpoint*. This word has the double advantage of containing a reference to "seeing" and of being more down to earth.

Starbucks thinks you can become a coffee connoisseur. Frank Perdue has a definite point of view on the best way to raise chickens: You need a tough man. Listerine isn't losing sleep over the fact that some people see it as a medicine-breath mouthwash. Its viewpoint is that medicine breath is Listerine's proof of efficacy. In its recent campaign, Sprite tried to establish a new rapport with young consumers by imposing its point of view that, for soft drinks, "Image is nothing, thirst is everything. . . ." Even Phileas Fogg, who travels the world to bring back new and exotic food ideas to the United Kingdom—Californian Tortillas, Pakora Potato Chips, Supercool Tortilla Chips,  and Punjab Puri, has a very definite opinion. Snacks are best when they're made in the United Kingdom. "Authentic snacks from around the world made in Medomsley Road, Consett," says the ad, not without humor. A last remnant of British imperialism.

These brands make their opinions heard. They express a point of view. Galaxy, in the United Kingdom, reminds true bons vivants, those who believe in indulging themselves, "Why should you have cotton when you can have silk?" In other words, to spoil themselves with the best. California Wine Coolers takes its name from the state where people know how to live the good life. This gives the brand a legitimate reason to play on many an American's stereotype by describing itself as "Just another reason to hate California."

Whether it's Frank Perdue or Phileas Fogg, Sprite or Galaxy, all these brands have formed an opinion and express it in their advertising. Which invests them with that much more character. Yet they are merely brands of packaged goods. Better, they're simply food products.

If a food product can adopt such a discourse, if it can go beyond the literal expression of benefit and offer the public a specific viewpoint, it's all the more feasible, not to mention justified, for a radio station, a vacation destination, or a sports-shoe brand. Radio FFN in Denmark recently aired the following message: "Tonight on TV, once again, lots of people are dying, simply for our entertainment. Really amusing. Dead funny. A suggestion: An evening without TV is an evening with no dead bodies, no murders, no horror, no blood, and no violence. There's great entertainment on the radio; 100 percent violence free." What a change from the usual self-promoting jingles of FM radio.

Club Med has a very clear idea of what vacation and leisure time should be. They have to serve as the "antidote to civilization." The Norwegian Cruise Line people share Club Med's point of view: "There is no law that says you can't make love at four in the afternoon on a Tuesday," they say, adding, "There is no law that says you should not study a sunset or train butterflies. There is no law that says you must pack worry along with your luggage. There is no law that says you must contribute to the GNP every day of your life." Norwegian Cruise Line makes cruises competitive with all other vacation alternatives through its viewpoint: Only cruises—the isolation inherent to a ship in the middle of the sea—are true escapes and therefore the ideal remedy.

Everyone remembers the English teacher from the movie *Dead Poets' Society*, and his speeches on nonconformity. The following voice-over sounds like something he would have said: "There is a time in every man's education when he arrives at the conviction that envy is ignorance, that imitation is suicide, that he must take himself for better or worse as his portion. Insist on yourself. Never imitate. . . . Society everywhere is in conspiracy against the manhood of every one of its members. To believe your own thoughts. To believe that what is true for you and your private heart is true for all men. That is genius!" While this may sound like something coming from Robin Williams, in fact it is the voice-over from a Reebok commercial that was aired a few years ago. The brand had a definite viewpoint on how to get off the beaten track. How to be yourself. "Reebok lets U.B.U."

Reebok takes a stand. Norwegian Cruise Line and Radio FFN do, as well. These brands define themselves. Same for Frank Perdue and Galaxy. They are out there saying something, expressing a point of view. For them, this is a way of calling attention to themselves, of finding an angle. Making your voice heard over the advertising din is becoming increasingly difficult. That is why raising the level of the discussion, adopting a new stance, is smart. It's easier to get yourself noticed for your opinions.

You shouldn't settle for saying what you are and what you do. You should say what you believe in. If you have a point of view, even people who don't agree with you will respect you because you stand for something. Having a point of view gives you direction. It connects you with people. That's why Disruption is about taking a stand. Brands need to have their very own way of looking at the world around them.

The Brand/Company Dynamic

Usually, a brand and a company are two totally different things. Nonetheless, in some cases, there is an interaction, a back-and-forth between the two. Let's look at a few scenarios.

When the Brand Is the Company Name

In many ways, this is the ideal situation for a brand. It draws strength from the firm's values, and in return, it embodies them, making them concrete.

For 30 years, BMW's engineers have both guided the company itself and the cars it produces. As a result, BMW has its own particular way of looking at the market, and a very strong corporate culture. Their engineers are motivated by one goal: Ensuring that their claim that no other car is as well thought out as a BMW is legitimate. That's truly the case. The people who design BMWs have very high ideals of what an automobile should be and the pleasure one should have driving one. They refuse to compromise and strive to make each model a masterpiece. Indeed, a BMW looks like no other car on the road. Their cars' originality consists in remaining absolutely true to the company vision that everything changes, nothing stays the same, except the BMW spirit. BMW, the company, never responds to demand. Rather, through the cars that bear its name, its engineers anticipate it.

France is the only country in the world where Apple is the predominant computer brand, both in terms of market share and consumer perception. Apple's launch campaign for Macintosh in France claimed: "It was about time a capitalist led a revolution." Numerous commercials followed. One shows a teacher of Morse code who suddenly understands he's out of a job: Edison has just invented the telegraph. Apple is to data processing what the telegraph was to Morse code.

In another commercial a rich Italian businessman gives his son a resolute speech on the virtues of being authoritarian with his employees. He explains that the workers are there to carry out orders and not to think. Otherwise, they'd want to change things, and this does not lie within the scope of their abilities. The voice-over of the ad concludes: "There are different ways of running a company. Here's one." The Apple logo appears on the screen. The voice-over continues: "Luckily, there are others."

Apple's richness of expression, variety of registers, and brilliant scripts are without equal. In France, Apple is not simply a brand of technologically revolutionary products. It's an antiestablishment company. The firm's values and the brand's values come together. They are indistinguishable from each other.

For certain companies, it is legitimate to have an ambitious vision. Ford, Wal-Mart, and Nestlé are well-known examples. They give the impression of knowing what share of the future they will have. But confident, inspirational raisons d'être are not only the domain of megabrands. Kindercare, for example, believes that child care is about stimulating the "whole child" and not just about school preparation. Gerber sees its baby foods as the closest thing to a mother's milk. And Rubbermaid, who by telling us for years that they work as hard as we do, instills a sense that its products will always be there to help us. It's hard to imagine a world without these brands. They're intransigent. When they speak to us, we sense what they'll be tomorrow.

McDonald's

McDonald's is currently the second-most-recognized brand in the world. After only 40 years of existence. McDonald's is an example of a company and a product that are inseparable.

In France, its success is only very recent. That's why I think it's interesting to discuss it in detail. Ten years ago, papers and magazines were teeming with articles condemning fast food. The capital of gastronomy and good eating regarded the advent of the hamburger with disdain. Some people referred to Disneyland's opening in France five years ago as nothing less than a "cultural Chernobyl." So it's easy to imagine the unkind words that journalists had used only a few years earlier to describe the leader of fast food's arrival.

In the mid-1980s, there was a profound change taking place in the parent-child dynamic in France. After years of parental authoritarianism, the parent-child relationship became more balanced. But this change was thwarted by everyday realities: lack of time, two working parents, television, and so on. While restaurants may have been the ideal setting for family gatherings far removed from daily constraints, the idea of family restaurants didn't exist. Traditional restaurants were reserved for adults who didn't need a special menu and who could be counted upon to be well mannered.

McDonald's filled this void. By being the first to portray and encourage this new parent-child sharing relationship, it projected an image of being the one restaurant that understood better than any other the societal changes that were taking place, much as McDonald's in the United States did when it validated a new generation of working mothers by telling them, "You deserve a break today."

The commercials reflect McDonald's belief that "it's kids who make their parents discover McDonald's." One of them shows children washing the family car to earn some money and, for the first time, taking their parents out to eat. Another commercial shows a very dignified older man being taken by his grandchildren to McDonald's, where he discovers the unexpected pleasure of eating good food with his hands. In another, a father is teaching his little girl how to ride a bike. When she finally gets her balance, she heads straight for McDonald's, with her father following in her wake.

The McDonald's restaurant itself also induced a feeling of shared pleasure and became a sort of "magic bubble," a relaxed fun atmosphere, where everyone leaves the worries of the outside world behind the minute he walks in the door. All of this is illustrated in a more recent commercial, entitled "Good Manners," in which a precocious child points out the adults around her who ignore proper table etiquette—a man with his elbows on the table, another reading his newspaper while eating, another stealing fries from his son, and even a young couple kissing. The child then tells us, with a smirk, "That's what it's like at McDonald's."

For the last 10 years, its advertising claim in France, "That's what it's like at McDonald's," has been a reflection of McDonald's vision. That McDonald's is a place unlike any other, that it's a place as much as a product. More important, that it's an experience. McDonald's is a universal meeting point for all ages and ethnic groups. It's as though McDonald's is a protected zone in which conflict and enmity don't exist. France is not free from underprivileged communities, which are typically suburbs on the outskirts of the larger cities. Like their inner-city American counterparts, life there is difficult and often marked by violence. Because McDonald's has become a refuge and meeting place void of aggression, many mayors of these suburbs have issued fervent pleas to McDonald's to open restaurants in their towns. Indicative of peace and calm—a fight has never broken out in one—the restaurants inspire other businesses to open nearby. More human town centers start to bloom.

Who could have imagined such a thing only a decade earlier? Who would have predicted that this would be McDonald's share of the future? Today, McDonald's enables people who had stopped talking to each other to start over. Who would have thought that McDonald's would be an agent of integration?

Ten years ago, there were only 20 McDonald's restaurants in France. Today there are almost 500. In five years, there will be close to 1,000. The country that was aghast at its arrival is now the very country in which McDonald's is experiencing tremendous growth. It's the favorite restaurant of 80 percent of French children.

Times have changed, in France and in the world. McDonald's in France now enjoys one of the most positive images of all its counterparts worldwide. What was once perceived as a mere fast-food joint has now become the family restaurant. There is McDonald's, and then there's the rest.

When the Brand Is Given Value by the Company Name

Trust in companies lends credit to the brand. Nowhere is that more true than in Japan, a very institution-oriented country where companies are revered. The Japanese trust them. This explains why a Japanese person always wants to know the name of the firm manufacturing the product he or she is buying.

The *noren effect* is the name the Japanese have given to this confidence. Long ago, *noren* signified the metal shade that a shop owner pulled down in front of the shop window at closing time with his name written on it in big characters. It symbolized the merchant's reputation. Today *noren* personifies the reputation of an entire company.

Because the brand and the company are so intertwined, it is often difficult to distinguish between Japanese institutional and product advertising. Far from hiding behind its brands, the company uses its name as both a reference and a signpost. The company is never anonymous. Western firms have taken note. They now even enlarge their logos on detergent and diapers sold in the Land of the Rising Sun.

Respect for great industrial and trade institutions is not limited to Japan. Great Britain, too, is home to a number of institutions, from Shell to BP, from Tesco to Sainsbury, from Boots to Lever. A study of their level of trustworthiness was recently conducted. Marks & Spencer came out in first place, with 85 percent of those surveyed favorably inclined, followed by Mars with 69 percent, and Ford with 65 percent. At the other end of the scale, politicians were granted a mere 13 percent.

Throughout the world, the general public is becoming wiser. Our contemporaries don't have to read the business pages of their favorite newspapers in order to understand the significance of corporations. You don't have to be an economic whiz to figure out the crucial role they play. People are more or less familiar with L'Oréal, Nestlé, and Unilever. And people buy the brands they offer because it's like a guarantee. Plenitude, Nescafé, and Lever 2000 are examples of brands that borrow from the reputation of the companies that manufacture them.

The result is that corporations are stepping into the limelight more and more. This trend is global and irreversible. When you rise to the corporate level, your discourse is enriched. Visions become clearer. Antoine Riboud has a very clear idea of the direction he wants BSN and its 70 umbrella brands to take. Recently, he changed BSN's name to that of Danone, the brand that best stands for the company's values. This is an original move. Here, a group borrows from its leading subsidiary, the one with the vision capable of carrying the entire company into the future. It's a loan of inestimable value.

When the Brand Acts as a Company

The worldwide sales figures of Oil of Olay and Tide are not published. But it's easy to have an idea of their magnitude. It would hardly be out of line to assume that their earnings fall within the range of those realized by a large corporation. In the U.S. market, there are currently 11 different products offered under the Tide name, and 25 under Oil of Olay. Brands such as these can be positioned as companies. Tide has the heft and reach of an institution—so much so that American women probably take it for a corporation. Tide, Inc.

Actually, many brands act as companies. First, there are those that in fact used to be companies and were taken over by larger ones, such as Orville Redenbacher. Then there are those that were the sole brand of a company that no longer exists and are now part of a larger conglomerate, such as Lysol. And those that are associated with tangible personae, such as Betty Crocker, Bartles & Jaymes, and Phileas Fogg, and that, de facto, come across

as firms. It is in these brands' best interests to
adopt a corporate discourse in their advertising. A company will always be endowed
with more depth than a simple brand.
The reasons for being loyal to them seem
more profound.

Finally, there are the more modern brands
that adopt corporate behavior. When M&M's
threw itself into an educational program with a highly corporate feeling, it
did so under its own name and not under the auspices of Mars Company.
When you think of Tropicana or Arm & Hammer in the United States, of
Findus or Lancôme in Europe, you have the impression they are corporations. The broadness of the line, the number of products covered, creates
this impression of size. All these brands could carry even greater weight.
They are not taking full advantage of their perceived status as companies.

Not long ago, we advised Reckitt & Colman to give Airwick in Europe
this breadth. To position it not as a brand of air freshener, but as the Air
Care Company. There are brands that for historical reasons strike one as
being bigger than the products that they comprise. They have everything
to gain from adopting a company profile.

"When you buy Tide, you're buying a product, not Procter & Gamble.
When you buy Nike, you're buying everything that goes with it," points
out Tom Peters. Maybe there is more to sell in Tide than simply the product. To do so would require raising Tide to the level of a company. The
Tide Company. You have a clear vision of what the Tide Company could
stand for. You have complete trust.

When General Motors wanted to produce something radically new, it
didn't design a new model but created a new company. Saturn is built on
a vision of the automobile that is radically different from GM's. It's not
simply about having technically competitive products but also a brand-
new sales and distribution approach. And a return to traditional American values. The advertising claim is quite simply, "A different kind of car,
a different kind of company."

When the Brand Is a Country

Like companies and products, a country's image has to be managed. When Poland handed Malcolm McLaren, the inventor of the punk movement, the controls of its image management, it was anything but ludicrous. Few people have ever had their antennae so finely tuned to their era as he has. McLaren doesn't just sense trends, he sees and creates them. On this issue, the French have also been forced to realize the importance of image management. As a result of negligence by the "powers that be," the country's image has deteriorated.

In many ways, people perceive countries as they do brands. They have their favorites and they know them well. After all, it's impossible to be intimate with each of the 184 registered members of the United Nations. So countries are known on only two or three dimensions. A country has a personality, a character, much like that of a brand. This is important. For just as there can be a correlation between a brand and its home company, the country's image can also influence the image of the brands produced in it.

The Danish Chamber of Commerce once asked my advice on how to improve Denmark's recognition in France to encourage an increase in exports. While few in France are capable of naming the second-largest city in Denmark, most know top Danish brands, such as Bang & Olufsen, Carlsberg, Velux, Lego, and Danfoss. My recommendation was to base Denmark's country image on the French perception of these brands: to capitalize on their being synonymous with all that is natural, beautifully designed, and timeless. The precise and positive image of each of these brands was thus transferred onto their country of origin and in turn served as a springboard for other Danish companies to penetrate the French market.

In the same way, Japan has capitalized on its homegrown brands for the past 20 years. Don't get me wrong: There aren't many Japanese brands that benefit from well-defined images. There are maybe a dozen, tops. But these very companies have given Japan a highly competitive reputation from which many of its firms have benefited. Thanks first to Honda, then to Sony and Seiko, in the 1960s and 1970s and later to Toyota and Nissan, Japanese industry is well known the world over. All other brands subsequently jumped on the bandwagon. They managed to take advantage of the image created by the leaders. Aiwa and Sanyo do not have any specific image. Their success is in part derived from their Japanese origin. Every Japanese brand now starts off with a basic and invaluable capital: the image of advanced Japanese technology.

Adopting an approach similar to that of Denmark or Japan would enable Danone, L'Oréal, Schlumberger, Peugeot, Renault, and Michelin to act as the ambassadors of French industry at large. The image of a country colors the image of a brand and vice versa. Because they realize that the reputation of French industry is mediocre, French firms that succeed abroad downplay their origins. Very few Japanese know that Michelin is French. How many Americans know the nationality of Dannon? This is why France should establish a vision of what it wants its industries to embody. It could stand for "industries that improve quality of life," an attribute that yogurts, high-speed trains, quality tires, the Concorde, as well as luxury goods such as wine and perfume, have in common. France has yet to capitalize on this opportunity and to realize that a great vision can project it into the future without forgetting the past.

A country with a vision provides its brands with an added competitive edge. From a European point of view, when you buy a pair of Nikes or Levi's, a pack of Marlboros, an IBM computer, a Chrysler minivan or simply a Coke, it's like buying a bit of the United States. The mythical and welcoming United States that, justifiably or not, still inspires dreams. *The Wall Street Journal* once played on this image: "For over three hundred years they've been coming. And while most haven't brought riches, they have brought dreams. At *The Wall Street Journal*, we believe that the most precious resources a country can have are the hopes of its people. Because tomorrow's achievements grow out of today's dreams." Each U.S. product carries with it a bit of the American dream. And it exports that dream with itself. That's one hell of an asset. That's unfair competition.

The Spirit of Coke

Diet Coke is a case in point of how a vision encompasses, precedes, and influences everything else. I had the occasion to chat about Diet Coke with Sergio Zyman. For me, Diet Coke's core question is what the brand's vision should be. For if you agree on the vision, everything else flows naturally. Our discussion was very thought provoking.

I believe that it's the Coke spirit that makes Diet Coke different. For this reason, it's the Coke, not the "Diet" part of Diet Coke that should be promoted. Coca-Cola and Diet Coke are two different products. But there's only one brand, with a lot of heritage and authenticity. Therefore, the messages that reassure about taste become irrelevant. Diet Coke needs to be more ambitious. It needs to make people think that when they're drinking a Diet Coke, they are having "the real thing."

> **"Though times may change, what's real stays the same."**

Coke has always been the real thing. It's always been about what's real and what matters. Something that you cannot see but that the whole world can feel. The "Always Coke" campaign abandoned this territory. Diet Coke can create an advantage by taking that back. And to the advantage of the Coke brand as a whole.

To a certain extent, Sergio Zyman agreed with us. He recently decided to stop selling Diet Coke as a diet product. But he didn't go all the way. He stopped at taste. He does not sell the spirit of Coke. I remain convinced that a return to the brand's historic vision is called for. And that the values Coke advocated during the 1960s and 1970s should be modernized. Adapted to today's issues, but with the same soul.

The Payoff of Strong Visions

"Patents expire. Copyrights expire. Only brands can be owned forever. If properly managed, brands can and do live forever," says Larry Light.

A brand is more than just a company's asset. It is a reference point for consumers. It transcends geography, adapting to diverse cultures, leading them to share the same expectations. A young Chinese person who wears a pair of Nikes, an Indian mother who drinks Evian, or a Mexican athlete who eats Dannon products are living proof of the universality and the healthy state of brands. They connect all people to each other. They make them share a way of life. Their legitimacy grows because they help people live together.

A brand's lifeblood is its vision. It's what guides that inextricable mix of the tangible and the intangible, to which the consumer is so attached.

Vision Builds Brand Value

On one hand, there's a brand's sentimental or emotional value, and on the other, its striking economic value. In 1984, Rupert Murdoch's group integrated its magazines into its overall balance sheet as intangible assets, in other words, as brands. In 1988, GrandMet did the same with the Smirnoff brand, which it had just purchased for £588 million. At the end of 1994, the Coca-Cola brand's worth was valued at $39 billion.

For Larry Light, the concept of *brand* has never been stronger than it is today. He points out that on Wall Street, stock market investors value a dollar of revenue growth twice as highly as a dollar of profit generated "through cost reduction." This finding appeared in a study involving more than 800 companies. The studies conducted by the Coalition for Brand Equity show that, on average, winning a new client is six times more costly than keeping a current one. And what is the loyalty of the latter based on? On the brand.

In the beginning, you create a product. Then you choose a brand name. Over time, the brand acquires its own value. It would be going a bit far to say it separates itself from the product, but it does distance itself. It takes on values that are often broader than the product itself. Danone, for instance, means a lot more than yogurt. The role of the agency is to think about these brand values. And to magnify them by including them in a long-term vision.

In the United Kingdom, the cornerstone of the Haägen-Dazs success story was a single, simple vision of the category: It's not just dessert but the ultimate in adult pleasure. Its advertising dramatizes the vision by showing seductive photographs of hot couples sharing cool delights, pure eroticism. This campaign has totally changed the perception of the ice cream category, allowing the brand to grow consistently since its launch five years ago, selling at a premium of 200 percent above the average price.

In the United States, Absolut is priced 50 percent higher than Smirnoff. Despite this price difference, Absolut has grown faster than the market itself. It did so by creating its own category: Absolut is not simply vodka, it's a spirit for people who are looking for uncompromised perfection. No other brand has generated more added value in this sector in the last 20 years. Absolut owes its success to the brilliance of its campaign and the incisiveness of its vision.

In 1989 TAG Heuer was known as a sports watch. Its ads were endorsed by sports celebrities such as Ayton Senna and Michael Schumacher. The brand was healthy. It boasted sales of $25 million, with the average price of a watch being $600. When TAG Heuer asked us "How can a sports brand become a luxury brand?," it knew that making this transition would mean higher profit margins and even increased overall sales.

There were two stages in this upgrading. The first, which corresponds to the "Don't crack under pressure" campaign, demonstrated the formidable concentration and self-control necessary to accomplish major athletic feats. The second stage, which has been on the air and in the pages of magazines for a year now, goes even further. As we've seen, the sportsperson creates powerful adversaries—sharks, sticks of dynamite, razor blades, 50-story abysses. The concept of mental strength has bridged the universe of sport and luxury. Mental effort is reconciled with prestige. TAG Heuer's sales have increased more than 200 percent in six years.

Even more impressive, the average price of a watch is now $1,100, an 80 percent increase over the same period. This obviously means much higher profits.

TAG Heuer succeeded in giving itself a vision. For TAG Heuer and many others, vision is what lends value to the brand. The vision repre-sents the future brand value.

Collins & Porras conducted a study that illustrated that brands are stronger when they are founded on long-term visions. To do so, they cre-ated a fictitious investment fund that simulated what would have hap-pened if one dollar had been invested in 1920 in over 200 American companies. For firms that were created post-1920, they invested the sum of a dollar plus the corresponding inflation coefficient for each year in between. At the same time, they separated visionary businesses from the rest based on a multitude of preestablished criteria. Over a period of 70 years, the visionaries outperformed their counterparts by a long shot. The gap was considerable. A correlation between success and vision was shown.

Collins & Porras were trying to illustrate what we know intuitively: If the vision is powerful, the brand is more energetic. It stands out from the crowd. It has greater value. In both senses of the word: Image value and fi-nancial value.

Vision Helps Brand Stretching

In *22 Immutable Laws of Marketing,* Ries and Trout categorically condemn line extensions. They list an impressive number of failures: Miller, General Electric, Slim-Fast, Adidas, and Heinz. In their view, if you don't make brand stretching an absolute no-no, you're bound for disaster. Here are just a few more examples: Johnson & Johnson Baby Oil's launch of a perfume, Pierre Cardin's foray into dishware, and Bic's venture into pantyhose.

Must one therefore condemn launching line extensions? I don't think so. Using existing brands to launch new products makes economies of scale possible. This answers an economic necessity. Moreover, the con-sumer's saturation level has been reached. Too many brands kill brands. Faced with their sheer number, the consumer might reduce them to empty names.

Brand extensions are inevitable. Yet because brand dilution can lead to commoditization, the brand must be upgraded even as it is extended. Hor-izontal extension. Vertical upgrading. Having a vision enables you to combine these two movements. It is because Danone succeeded in elevating its image with the health-oriented message of yogurt that it could get away with launching all those desserts.

The agency should act as the brand's guardian. The more the brand is stretched, the more carefully it must be managed. Putting time on your side and taking a compass reading of where you are headed are critical. We have developed several seminars on brand stretching. The first one deals with a brand's architectural makeup. Another addresses the pitfalls to avoid. A third explores the role of pillar products as symbols of the brand. Proper management of a brand's elasticity is a delicate process.

Launching flankers does not dilute brands. On the contrary, if newcomers are in line with the brand's vision, they fortify it. Danone launched Bio yogurt, with its active bifidus cultures and depurative benefits, with the claim "what it does on the inside is visible on the outside." This in turn strengthened Danone's health-oriented image even more. It nourished it.

This illustrates the issue of the relationship between an umbrella brand and the products it comprises. Something to be managed with great care every step of the way. Examining each case individually. In the Mars group, for example, brands have different extension possibilities. They probably even vary from one country to the next. The Mars bar is difficult to stretch. It's closely connected to its original recipe. It is not easy for the bar to transcend its physical origin. On the other hand, Snickers has succeeded masterfully at this undertaking. Of all the leaders in the candy bar market, Snickers managed to transform itself and become in the space of a few months the leading brand of ice cream bar in the United States. In the case of Galaxy, because it owns a very broad territory, indulgence, it can also cover a great number of products, such as Galaxy Truffle Hearts, Galaxy Ripple, Galaxy Double Nuts and Raisins, Galaxy Caramel, Galaxy Minstrels, and so on.

Europe boasts more umbrella brands than the United States. Because populations are smaller and per capita spending is lower, individual country's brand billings are inferior. Limits are reached quite quickly. The funds necessary for launching a new brand are often lacking. Critical mass is not reached. So the only solution is to fit under existing brand.

In "What Happened to Madison Avenue," Martin Mayer pointed out what he considers to be a handicap for Americans. In his eyes, "Europeans have internalized, and Americans haven't, the knowledge that products have life cycles, but brands don't." However, things have begun to change in the United States. During the last five years, seminars on overbranding have come into vogue. Company heads are trying to get more out of their existing business. As a result, in 1992 and 1993, more than 75 percent of new products in the United States were launched under an existing brand. They can't all be wrong.

In fact, if a new product is in line with the brand's vision, it will always give the brand a new spurt of energy. It will demonstrate the brand's vitality. McCain in Europe is a good example of brand stretching done in an unconventional way. When manufacturers want to buy brands to grow their businesses, the price is most often prohibitive. Multiples of 25, even 30 or more, are frequent. While a brand's price is exorbitant, factories can be purchased dirt cheap. So, McCain decided to grow by acquiring factories and applying its know-how in industrial engineering to rapidly increase their productivity. It's then up to marketing and communications to integrate the diverse products McCain produces into one unified brand identity. One strong and broad enough to follow McCain's rapid rhythm of expansion.

Today, McCain products include fries, other potato-based specialties, green vegetables, desserts, prepared dishes, orange juices, iced teas, and hors d'oeuvres. McCain has been able to hop from one market to another. In France, its sales have multiplied tenfold in five years. Its success is the result of its belief that you don't have to be gourmet in the French sense of the word to be good. In other words, McCain has taken it upon itself to champion the impossible: putting American food in French homes. McCain is proof that a generalist does not have to be as vulnerable as marketing experts often think.

Virgin is another example of a brand that spans many different businesses. Once a record label, it has become a retailer of cultural products (with 16 megastores across the globe) and electronics equipment (stereos, videos, home computers), an airline, a tour operator, as well as an audio-visual, literary, and video game production company, and even a brand of condoms. It's recently launched its own cola brand, Virgin Cola. Of all the brands I'm familiar with, Virgin is among the most stretchable. It's a strong, powerful brand based on a real vision. It can thus handle branching out into many different sectors.

Virgin owes its vision to the iconoclastic, irreverent man at its helm who set out to battle set ways and fixed ideas. With an agenda that is at once specific and unlimited, Richard Branson renders the inconceivable conceivable. Who would have thought that someone who started his career with Mike Oldfield's "Tubular Bells" would be feared by British Airways and Air France 20 years later? In Virgin, we find the cult of difference and nonconformity as much as an instinct for opportunities and demonstrative leadership behavior. That's what makes it the symbol and the reflection of a whole generation. Virgin always addresses the same audience and makes the very most of this focus. It plays on its synergies. Each product or service complements the next. The campaign for the launch of Virgin in the United States showed Phil Collins wearing his Walkman headphones in a Virgin plane. Similarly, there are plane ticket reservation windows in the megastores of London and Tokyo.

As far as Virgin is concerned, worrying about whether or not brand extensions are justified is outdated. It's anachronistic.

Vision Helps Rejuvenate the Brand

When a new agency opens for business, many clients bring it their problem brands. It's one way of testing the agency. And if the brand is in really bad shape, nothing is at stake. It's like giving the brand one last chance. That is what happened to BMP and CDP in the United Kingdom during the 1960s and 1970s. It is what happened to us during our first few years. Having dealt with many problem brands and helping to turn them around, we have seen that the more powerful the vision is, the more the brand is likely to be rejuvenated.

For example, we turned Caprice des Dieux, an outdated processed cheese, into a contemporary one by transforming it into a simple snack food and adapting it to laid-back lifestyles. Kronenbourg's beer, 1664, too, was falling asleep on its pedestal. We gave it new life by infusing it with a touch of eroticism. These brands rejuvenated their visions of themselves and experienced an upturn in sales.

There are also several notable brands in the United States that are as strong today as they were over 50 years ago, but not without many bumps and bruises along the way. Take, for instance, products as different as Crayola crayons and Ritz crackers. By diversifying their offer, adding more colors and new shapes, and by launching new products that transcended each company's traditional market definition, both have experienced an intense, pure rejuvenation over the past five years. Today, Crayola products are no longer just about coloring but about being the child's imagination partner. Similarly, Ritz crackers are more than the perfect cracker, they're now the perfect snack anytime.

Some brands have been around for years, but Americans feel as though they've discovered them only yesterday. Take, for example, Rolling Rock beer and Ocean Spray cranberry juice. Rolling Rock changed its bottle and Ocean Spray celebrated its tangy taste. As a result, Rolling Rock became a status symbol of the yuppie generation and Ocean Spray, the ideal source for out-of-this-world refreshment.

There are also dozens of brands whose images became blurred or seemed to disappear over time and then 20 years later suddenly reappear, unchanged, yet appear current and up to date. Think about just a few: Puma, Keds, Tastycake snacks, Birkenstocks, Oshkosh B'gosh, even Ovaltine or, in Europe, Omo detergent, Laughing Cow cheese, and Nivea skincare products.

When citing brands that have been around forever and have enjoyed a veritable renaissance, you can't forget to mention Arm & Hammer baking soda. Its repositioning as the single most powerful refrigerator deodorizer enabled it to later cast itself as the only brand of baking soda with the most effective natural whitening and deodorizing ingredient available. Today, Arm & Hammer has products in more than 15 different categories.

Let's move to the United Kingdom and look at two institutions that have managed to become current again: Guinness and *The Economist*. Guinness, though a much loved brand, and by far the leading stout, was being consumed less and less frequently, especially by younger drinkers, who preferred lighter and more exotic foreign beers. By the early 1980s, its share of the United Kingdom draft beer market was below 4 percent and plummeting. It had become an older people's drink. Instead of aiming for mainstream appeal, Guinness decided to create a unique vision of its product as the nonconformist or "intellectual" pint. The "Guinness—Pure Genius" campaign stages strange themes such as telepathy, extraterrestrials, dolphins, and so on. They are esoteric and serve the tag line, "Guinness—Pure Genius." Such a claim and everything that it implies captured the attention of young drinkers who saw in Guinness a new way of expressing their own individualism. They started to drink it again.

The Economist is also an illustration of the power of a new vision. Founded in the mid-nineteenth century as a current affairs and business journal, some years ago it seemed like little more than the last of a dying breed. It was no longer seen as compulsory reading for businesspeople, who preferred to keep themselves informed with a diet of up-to-the-minute news from the daily papers or news networks. In such a context, the magazine was suffering from a steady decline in readership and advertising revenue. The new perspective which resuscitated *The Economist* was to not simply be a useful source of information but to be "the badge of intelligence." This new vision transformed the magazine itself. It has gone from being a dry, almost academic journal to one that covers timely subjects with its own particular style and humor. The advertising is a reflection of this. New readers were won over by ad headlines such as "It's lonely at the top, but at least there's something to read." And "Behind every *Economist* reader there's someone who isn't." And "If more women read *The Economist*, there'd be fewer jobs for the boys." A more recent ad bears a quote for its headline: "I never read *The Economist*." It's signed "Management trainee. Aged 42 . . ." The fruit of this new vision has been a 30 percent rise in readership and a rapidly increasing share of younger age groups.

In France, no brand had a thicker layer of dust on it than the savings bank known as the Caisses d'Epargne, created in 1818 by French aristocrats with the philanthropic goal (at least that's what they claimed at the time) of giving the working class a place to put its savings. For the past 10 years, the Caisses d'Epargne has offered all the services of a modern bank. But few people are aware of it. Some have no idea that the Caisses d'Epargne allows you to have a checkbook or even a bankcard. For many, it's nothing more than a place to put your savings. The historical background of the institution has left its mark.

To rejuvenate the Caisses d'Epargne, we had to come up with a new vision. Because banks are usually patronizing, the Caisses d'Epargne decided to speak to the public with a different voice and not to have a teacher-student discourse. To avoid condescension and stiff, formal language.

Its press campaign is done in a surprisingly jarring way. In one magazine spread, the visual is a close-up shot of a boxer. His face is full of anguish, sweat is dripping from his brow, and his fists are cocked in front of him as he receives a sharp blow to the right side of his face. The headline is a question: "Take your salary. Reduce it by half. Now, how does it feel to be retired?"  Another ad depicts a blond, round-cheeked baby like the one on the Gerber babyfood label. The question here is: "Is this the only person who makes it possible for you to pay fewer taxes?" In a third, the visual shows a prison cell photographed through the bars, with this question: "What does an apartment that you can't pay off look like?" From one ad to the next, the questions continue: "When someone offers you the investment of the year, are you sure that it will be next year's, too?" And, "Do you know many people who dream of being tenants?" Or even a photo of a pregnant woman on one side and on the other the question "For the moment, your child has his own room, but in nine months will he still have one?" Quite an intrusive campaign for such a staid institution. All these headlines reflect the questions that people actually ask themselves. The Caisses d'Epargne campaign makes them realize that these are the right ones.

What do all these brands and companies have in common? What about McCain, *The Economist,* or Caisses d'Epargne? When you look at the way these brands present themselves to the consumer today, you get the feeling that they're in control. They are built on solid visions. They show vitality. They have stretched themselves beyond traditional market segments by adding new products. They use advertising as a fast and powerful agent of change. They have understood that vision means being a little ahead of reality.

All too often, advertising ties itself to an existing image and merely strives to strengthen the brand's roots. We get bogged down in the values of the past, failing to see that our clients expect us to produce change and want us to help them see their brands or companies in a new light. Advertising must serve as an accelerator for sculpting new visions.

Legitimacy

The question "Is the message credible?" often arises. Yet for me the more pertinent question to ask is "Is the message legitimate?"

All you have to do is watch TV in the evening and you'll see that credibility is a moot point. We never ask ourselves whether or not the Coca-Cola, Nike, or TAG Heuer campaigns are credible. By contrast, we might question the extent to which a brand raises certain issues. The legitimacy issue is far more germane. Apple's antiestablishment discourse could not have been adopted by just any brand. Nike refused to accept the limits that other brands will never get beyond. Saturn went so far as to set up shop in Tennessee to legitimize its discourse on traditional American values.

It's no small feat taking a stand, as these brands do. What allows a brand to change the playing field? How does a brand go about building its legitimacy? You either have to aim high right from the start or put time on your side.

From the very birth of their brands, and in some cases years before they even advertised, Phil Knight, Sam Walton, and Ralph Lauren knew ahead of time what they wanted to do and what path they were going to take. They saw no limit to what their brands could one day mean. It's what makes them true entrepreneurs.

From its inception, Ralph Lauren clothing embodied classic New England. Now, whatever product he offers, whatever store he designs, whatever perfume he launches, as long as it is in keeping with the Old Money/New England imagery, it will be a success. Ralph Lauren imposed his brand's legitimacy. Calvin Klein did the same, albeit in a more daring arena. It is impossible to imagine the sensuality of Eternity or the eroticism of Obsession coming from Hermès or Guerlain. It's the sender's personality that makes the message acceptable. For brands from Calvin Klein to Wal-Mart, vision precedes everything else. It is the founding act. It legitimizes all the subsequent initiatives that are taken in its name.

More often than not, however, legitimacy is built up gradually. Certain brands' takeoffs are not quite as clear-cut. A brand's history, its advertising, and the initiatives it has taken throughout the years are what entitle it to take a new stand. That's what happened with Virgin in France. Today, Virgin can confront many of the issues facing young people—even battles as large as taking on the French sacred cow, a law that requires all stores to remain closed on Sundays. It was only Virgin's proof that it was not just a store, but a provider of culture, that enabled it to prevail. After all, if museums are open for the public's enrichment on Sundays, why should music be off-limits? In the same way, Pepsi did not become the choice of a new generation in a day. It took 25 years to create. In the struggle for legitimacy, sometimes it's worth knowing how to put time on your side.

Two salesmen selling competing brands meet in a diner. Each makes the other try his brand. The first one hands back the product of the second one. The second, won over, refuses to give his competitor his product back. No creative I know would dare propose a storyboard of such pathetic banality.

Joe Pytka ended up filming this scene and won a Lion d'Or at the Festival de Cannes. When you add to the storyboard that the first salesman sells Pepsi and the second sells Coke, it becomes one of the most powerful commercials aired in years. Pytka's talent alone does not explain the impact of this commercial. It's the historic, yet never-ending, battle between Pepsi and Coke that made it possible. For 25 years, and since the Pepsi Challenge, Pepsi has given itself legitimacy, which is strengthened commercial after commercial. Incisive, comparative, funny commercials that combine the best of advertising by allying the hard with the soft sell. Pepsi's impertinence is what made it the choice of each new generation. Today, I can't think of any other brand that could have gotten away with a commercial like this one.

The Union Bank of Switzerland has been around since 1912. Stability is its commercial foundation. Like many Swiss institutions, it sells itself on its solidity, its capacity to simply go through decades and endure crises. This vision is that wisdom is derived from unutterable durability. This is translated through a very unusual pan-European campaign. Shot in dark monochromatic tones, the campaign features the shadowed profiles of celebrated British thespians reciting timeless and classic poems—John Gielgud doing "A Tide in the Affairs of Men" from Shakespeare's *Julius Caesar* and a passage from Tennyson's "Ulysses," Alan Bates reciting Robert Frost's "The Road Not Taken," and Ben Kingsley sharing with us a poem from the romantic Shelley. Each poem is more than just a mere performance, it is a highbrow communication of the notions of enduring human values. Not surprisingly, the end line sums up UBS' credo: "Thoughts that transcend time."

You have to be a Swiss institution to make such a claim. The Union Bank of Switzerland anchors itself in the past. By contrast, the number two mail-order company in France, the 3 Suisses, inscribes itself in today's actuality. Yet the 3 Suisses also manages to create its own legitimacy.

Magazines are full of articles about the emergence of feminine values. They're full of the usual right-brain commonplaces. In one, a journalist, paraphrasing Malraux, declares that the twenty-first century will be feminine or won't exist. Brands interpret these articles literally and then extract their ideas to give their advertisements substance. Easily borrowed and awkwardly used. Ads about feminine values, whether they're for clothing, perfume, even cars or cigarettes, are usually little more than a collection of banalities. Facetious repetition.

This is not the case when 3 Suisses takes the floor. For the past seven years, its advertising has valorized womanhood without falling into the vacuous clichés. As a result, the brand has acquired a certain authority and is seen as possessing a special sensitivity. The 3 Suisses has become more than just a mail-order company. It is now the brand that has the greatest affinity with women.

Its latest campaign proclaims that *"Demain sera féminin"*. Loosely translated, "Tomorrow will be feminine." Coming from 3 Suisses, the theme has a special resonance. There is no feeling that it's borrowed. Everything the 3 Suisses has to say seems natural. The campaign tells us that "A woman has never set foot on the moon. There's still so much to do down here." It raises questions such as "What if we stopped teaching little boys that only girls cry?" When 3 Suisses speaks in such a way, it is legitimate. Anything it says about feminine values is valid.

Talking to a Target That Refuses to Be a Target

Establishing legitimacy is a way—perhaps the only way—to talk to a generation that hates the idea of being a target.

The younger generations have always had advertising in their lives. They instantly decode its messages. They know what makes an ad tick. It's not that they reject advertising as a whole. It's just that there are some approaches they can't stand. They hate being labeled. They refuse the idea of being described. They never recognize themselves in the image advertisers try to project of them. The identification route no longer works. And it hasn't for a long time. In Nike, Levi's, and the new Coke commercials, you never see the target. And when you do, as in the Pepsi ads, they never try to be realistic. They're funny and slightly offbeat.

While the target is distrustful of advertising, young people still like brands. Not necessarily those of their parents. But with just as much fervor. They like brands that know how to speak to them. Brands that spurn manipulative haranguing and stereotyping. Brands like CK One, Body Glove, Unlisted, Vans, and Diesel. Cool brands.

Advertisers who want to address today's youth and be heard don't have a lot of leeway. They have to find the right tone if they want to get across the bridge. Speak more simply. Address the issues as they are, without beating people over the head or being grandiloquent. With authenticity.

MTV

Legitimacy is essential and will only become more so in the future. The younger generations do not accept lies and imitations. That is why they like MTV. In their eyes, MTV represents a lot more than a mere provider of music videos. It's the only network that addresses the issues and interests of teens and young adults across the globe. Empowered as both the voice and reflection of today's youth, MTV has become politically and socially active worldwide, promoting issues ranging from antidrug and safe sex to battling racism and encouraging the Middle East peace process. When music videos are interspersed with public-service announcements that convey messages such as "You can never be too rich, but you can be too prejudiced" or tell you to "Free your mind and speak your mind," to "Rock against drugs," or to "Please use a condom," viewers listen. When MTV created the "Rock the Vote" campaign and program that documented the 1992 election, voters aged 18 to 24 turned out in the highest numbers in a long time. MTV even takes things down to a more personal level, encouraging simple human interaction. One announcement says "Spend some time with the one you love." MTV also encourages intergenerational solidarity by creating a program through which young people help senior citizens.

Who would have dreamed in the mid-1980s that one day MTV would turn into a kind of moral authority? Its legitimacy was cultivated gradually. Its public-service announcements are produced with the same talent as their best videos. The writing is sharp, polished, intrusive. Colorful, too. On a broader scale, MTV can allow itself to play the role of educator and authority figure precisely because every aspect of MTV is designed not to be authoritative, but rather communal, shared. . . . MTV is all about youth speaking to youth, banding together to muddle through typical growing pains and learning to become responsible and fulfilled adults.

MTV was legitimate from its inception, thanks to its raison d'être: music. However, that didn't ensure automatic acceptance of its educational ads. It was their flair and the intelligent writing that did. Didactic and moral tones are absent. No smugness. Young people aren't hung up on the fact that MTV is teaching them a lesson. MTV put itself in a position that enables it to talk to them this way. What is has to say is authentic.

I believe that advertisers who need to reach young people should look to MTV for inspiration. They need to find a tone that validates their stand. Having a product to sell is not in itself a justification. Even if an advertising message's content isn't lofty, it still needs to be authentic. Sincere. When Malcolm McLaren came to BDDP one day, he commented that "Advertising has to get rid of its penchant for manipulative discourse."

For some, this requires a good deal of effort. For others, such as Levi's, Solo, Mars, and Kookai, it comes naturally.

Levi's advertising in Europe is an outstanding example of creating legitimacy. By rewriting the history of the evolution of jeans, BBH's commercials bring the Levi's myth up to date. Their unexpected vignettes that explain how jeans came to be throw new light on the brand. They take something old and make it new. If indeed teenagers have their own world, no one embodies it better than Levi's. By a long shot. Fifteen years ago, Levi's had lost a lot of ground in Britain. BBH has given it back its pedigree. John Hegarty, BBH's chairman, sums it up: "We sell the land where the teenager was born."

The search for authenticity reflects a desire for no nonsense. An understated echo of this comes to us from Norway, where Solo, the local orange soft drink, succeeded in beating off the challenge of Pepsi and Coke by deflating the slick aspirational images so common in soft drink advertising. Each ad tells the story of a character in difficulty. He or she takes a swig of Solo and . . . the problem still remains. In one commercial, a cyclist in a race struggles to bike up a mountain pass. He takes a swig of Solo and . . . is still at the rear of the pack. Same thing for the wallflowers at a dance: Even after a glass of Solo, they're still not asked to dance. The number of conceivable situations is infinite. At the end of each commercial, the caption flashes on the screen: "The only soft drink which cures nothing but thirst."

These campaigns express the spirit of their day. They talk to the MTV generation. Like the Kookai campaign in France. Kookai is to French teens what The Limited is to their American counterparts. Yet there are probably few American retailers who would dare to celebrate a teen's seductive nature to such an extent. "Hide your boyfriends. I'm coming," says an impudent sweet young thing. "Summer's going to be hot, especially for the boys," says another. "All the boys in my class flunked, and it's all my fault," says a third sassy girl. Kookai depicts a slightly off-center vision of fashion. Its slogans are pertinent and insightful. They have made the brand immediately likable and legitimate. Kookai can dare anything. Like being endorsed by major couturiers. "All these girls in Kookai, that's not good. I'm not saying that for myself, but for the other designers," says Karl Lagerfeld, whose photo constitutes the visual for one ad. Similarly, Yves Saint Laurent says, "Kookai? I've heard people talking about them, but I've never seen one personally." Or Sonia Rykiel: "Kookaism will never wear out." Kookai plays with the common, everyday references of a young world. It has transformed its insolence into its legitimacy. The little ready-to-wear brand with its 300-franc short-sleeved blouses has put haute couture in its pocket. Talent can open many doors.

It took Kookai's advertising five years to move from a photo of a 13-year-old nymphet to a portrait of Karl Lagerfeld. Before coming up with the fifth-pocket ad, BBH produced 18 commercials in order to fashion, little by little, the current imagery of Levi's. The richness of the 3 Suisses, UAP, and Danone campaigns did not occur overnight. The Pepsi Challenge is 20 years old. Legitimacy most often is built slowly. As Cervantes said, "You have to let time take its time."

Benetton's Missed Opportunity

Luciano Benetton has a vision. Olivero Toscani, his photographer, interprets it. Unlike many people, I don't disapprove of Benetton's initiatives. Quite the contrary. Yet, I feel that Benetton doesn't make good use of the legitimacy he's established.

Benetton's provocative posters are well known, criticized, and controversial the world over. Many see in them only facile opportunism and shamelessness. For these people, AIDS, racism, homosexuality, and religion are guarded domains and certainly not those of a clothing manufacturer. Luciano Benetton thinks the opposite. He has money, so why not put it to work for the important issues of our times? Condemning his initiative is, in his view, a sign of outdated morality.

Undeniably, there is something generous in taking on the issues of our day. Many artists and sociologists are on his side. My take on this lies elsewhere. Benetton should focus on one issue: the fight against racism. Nothing else. You can't take on all causes at once.

With the "United Colors of Benetton," this Italian brand became a global spokesman on the topic. Images speak louder than words, and Benetton succeeded in rendering interracial exchange and understanding concrete. In this realm, Benetton is unquestionably legitimate, while in the other issues it addresses, such as AIDS and homosex-

uality, it is not. For us, it's normal that Benetton talks about racism. We don't bat an eye now but that wasn't the case in his company's early days.

If you take a step back, you might even wonder how a brand of sweaters, however colorful they are, could have come so far as to have made such an impact on a nonbusiness issue. It took a lot of talent.

A charming anecdote reflects this. Ten years ago, the Champs Elysées was lined with posters showing a young American boy holding the Soviet flag and a young Russian girl waving the Star-Spangled Banner. They were both smiling at us. As Gorbachev descended the avenue to the sound of applause, he leaned toward Mitterrand and asked, "Who is this Mr. Benetton?" Multiracialism, interracial unions, and peace among different peoples had become a legitimate discourse for Benetton. That's far from nothing. Yet I would have preferred to see the brand supporting Nelson Mandela before the end of apartheid or, today, helping to carry humanistic writer Maya Angelou's message around the globe, or forcing the world to look at the explosions of racism in Bosnia, Kashmir, and Rwanda. By doing so, Luciano Benetton would get better use out of the platform he had the intelligence to create.

He seems to possess a clear image of a world without interracial hatred. That is the most beautiful vision one can have. Everyone's future depends on it. It's a shame that his voice has gone flat.

Looking through a Telescope

Apple opposes, IBM solves, Nike exhorts, Virgin enlightens, Sony dreams, Benetton protests. . . . I believe Dan Wieden said that brands are not nouns but verbs.

A brand is powerful only if it takes action. And only if that action moves the brand toward its vision. The public remembers with greater clarity brands that know where they're going. There is a correlation between the existence of a vision and the awareness of a brand. The vision brings the brand closer to us. Brands with visions don't address the customer or the consumer. They address the person behind it. That's why we like them.

A vision often comes from an individual. An entrepreneur. Whether it's Steve Jobs or Phil Knight, Lou Gerstner or Sam Walton. They make their companies and the whole world share the values to which they are attached. They do not speak to a mass of consumers. They speak to each and every one of us.

In order to define a vision, the entrepreneur brings together two worlds. His inner world and the world around him. His imagination confronts reality. If the two meet, the brand will be strong.

When you close your eyes, you see your inner world. When you open them, you see the outside world as it presents itself. If you keep one eye open and the other one closed, your sight is blurred, but you find your vision.

When you look through a telescope, you have to close one eye if you want to see farther.

PART III
DISRUPTION
IN PRACTICE

A marketing approach cannot exist only in theory. The first chapter in Part III, "Disruption Methodology," explains how Disruption has been transformed into a living language used at each step of the strategic process to get to the end result: disruptive advertising campaigns. The following chapter, "Disruption Sources," further details the types of disruptions that brands and companies can create for themselves and explains how, by doing so, they can alter their places in their respective markets.

7

DISRUPTION
METHODOLOGY

AS EARLY AS 1899, the director of the U.S. Patent Office in Washington, D.C., declared that everything there was to invent had already been invented. Many people continue to claim there are no more new ideas. That opinion has become a commonplace.

However, advertising agencies insist that they are still coming up with ideas, which they refer to as either *selling* or *creative* ideas. For agencies, an idea is not a concept or an abstract representation. Agencies' ideas have to do with business, with life. Agencies use the term in the broad sense. For them, an *idea*, as defined in the dictionary, is a particular way of representing the world, of seeing things.

It is not easy to explain how ideas are born. Suddenly, someone looks at something in a way no one has seen before. The idea springs forth, as though by accident.

Lewis Carroll described it beautifully in *Symbolic Logic:* "Once upon a time, a coincidence went out for a stroll in the company of a little accident. While they were walking," he continued, "they met an explanation, a very old explanation. So old, in fact, that it was all bent over and wrinkled, and looked rather like a riddle. . . ."

You can spend hours on end studying an analysis or an explanation without ever being the least bit inspired. But an idea must come from somewhere. It is up to you to create the accident or bring about the coincidence that will make it come forth. One thing leads to another. An association of ideas creates something new and unexpected. That's the accident: You see a relationship that nobody has seen before.

Companies should be places where novel ideas are sparked and brought together. The more often this is the case, the more creative and, consequently, more successful your business will be. The role of any manager is to maximize the chances for such accidents to happen. Synectics Corporation, an international consultancy firm in Cambridge, Massachusetts, believes that each company must learn how to "take an accident and turn it into a process."

When an agency compiles a cassette of its creative commercials to represent the entirety of its production, there is an element of randomness in the commercials it chooses. Moreover, every agency has clients for which it creates commercials deemed "creative" and commercials for other clients that are not. This very fact, however, becomes masked by this infamous agency reel, which, by virtue of its selective nature, creates the illusion that it is indicative of the overall creativity of the agency. Agencies share only their best case histories and act as if the mediocre doesn't exist. The reality remains that every agency, some to a larger extent than others, needs to improve its creative hit rate.

As the poet Jacques Prévert said, "Chance doesn't occur by chance alone." There is a need to develop processes that improve the odds of creative output, processes that serve as catalysts for developing creative ideas and are open-ended enough to stimulate rather than hinder new associations of ideas.

You cannot start from nothing. Creativity cannot occur in a vacuum. Learn about the consumers, interpret their habits, decode their behaviors. Understand the client, as well. Decipher the company culture, and grasp the client's way of viewing the market. Know what your client does and does not know. Recognize the differences between facts and opinions. All of these actions gradually prepare the mind to be open to novelty, to look for accidents—those new combinations of ideas that trigger something.

Tools for Associating

The times we live in make it critical for us, and especially our profession, to remain open, to enrich ourselves from the experiences of others, and to be attentive to everything. Curiosity should be the defining characteristic of good advertising people. Every facet of life should interest us. There is nothing under the sun that does not merit our attention. We should be, as Tom Peters suggests, "curiosity workers."

Curiosity is about drawing inspiration from others. The greatest men and women don't hesitate to do it. "The Louvre is the book that teaches us to read," said Cézanne. Indeed, when Monet met Degas, the latter was seated on a bench in the Louvre, copying one of Velasquez's *infantas*. They weren't the only ones seeking inspiration from the past. Dozens of eighteenth- and nineteenth-century engravings are testimony to this. The Louvre was at once a school and a studio. Seats were expensive. To find a place to paint, you had to climb over a forest of easels.

I like to flip through books on advertising and the *Art Directors Annuals*. Rummaging around in this sundry bunch of posters, commercials, and print ads is always very inspiring. A headline here, a visual there, and you're under the spell. Your imagination soars.

When we began our work on a campaign for UAP, the largest insurance company in France, a planner came upon a print ad for Cadillac, written by a talented copywriter in 1921, with the headline, "The Penalty of Leadership." This headline encapsulated the idea that, whatever its field, a leader should never behave like the rest of the pack. It must throw itself into question. It must have an insatiable desire to do more. This curious planner recognized that Cadillac had expressed the raison d'être of a leader, that same truth that UAP wanted to convey to the French public. Without the inspiration from the Cadillac ad, the UAP campaign would never have created the impact it did.

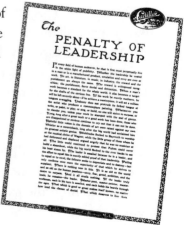

One of the commercials shows maternity wards circa 1945, nurseries with hundreds of babies, and headlines announcing the baby boom. The commercial then becomes a time line on which the years 2000, 2010, and 2015 pass by. An eight-column newspaper headline declares, "The Granny Boom." The voice-over explains: "In the year 2010, the baby boom generation will retire . . . having done it all—rock 'n' roll, demonstrations, aerobics, and the race for success—they will have 30 years and plenty of plans ahead of them. The 'granny boom' will be their veritable second life. As long as each one of them has a monthly income and that income is guaranteed for life. It's not easy. But you're either number one or you're not." Then the voice-over gives proof of its assertion by explaining that UAP not only diagnoses but proposes retirement plans that match each individual's needs like no other insurance company does.

The risks that small and medium-size companies confront became the subject of another commercial. In a factory, a horde of bottles is coming down the assembly line. There are hundreds of them. Some of them teeter slightly on the conveyor belt. Suddenly we notice that one bottle is different from all the others—it already has a gold cap on it, while the others have none. The voice-over declares, "It doesn't take much to kill a company. Does that surprise you?" The capped bottle then breaks, upsetting the flow of all the others. A second and third bottle break. Then, like a house of cards, all the bottles crash to the floor. The voice-over informs us, "Most companies are insured for accidents, not their consequences. You can avoid all this by anticipating, calculating, and covering every single risk." The factory lights shut off. "It's not easy," we are told, "but you're either number one, or you're not." A sentence proposing UAP's Industrial Multirisk Insurance appears on the screen: "One company, one contract, for fully comprehensive coverage."

This campaign's originality lies in its tension. That tension exists in each commercial. Broadly stated, a problem is presented. One that seems difficult to solve, almost impossible. One that requires a more-than-expected effort on the part of the insurer. The voice-over gives the impression that it cannot be done. You sense the difficulty, the obstacles to overcome, the challenge. Therein lies the tension. When UAP pronounces "It's not easy, but you're either number one, or you're not," it's a call to action. Thanks to it, the message is taut, as is the effort.

The Ricochet Effect

When the UAP campaign was at the briefing stage, the Cadillac ad was presented. Until then, the brief had been conventional. It was nothing more than a banal leadership strategy. The headline of the Cadillac ad served as the accident, the source of inspiration.

This anecdote is anything but incidental. It illustrates a way of working. The collective experience of thousands of advertising professionals who, for 20 or 30 or more years, have managed to find original solutions to problems is an inestimable treasure. I think every member of our staff should be erudite when it comes to advertising. It is always useful to look at examples, to pick up insights other people have, and to see if there is something we can bounce off of. A campaign for a bank in Singapore might suggest an idea for a more inspiring brief for a beverage in Spain. It's not a question of imitation but of ricochet. The key is understanding that, through a new association of ideas, one execution in a product category can lead you to discover a new entry, a new angle—even a new strategy. On the execution level, the UAP campaign is totally unrelated to the Cadillac campaign. But the logic underlying the two messages is the same.

Chance does favor the prepared mind. Indeed, if we hadn't intuitively known what we were looking for, we never would have found inspiration in "The Penalty of Leadership."

The Disruption World Bank

In large international agencies, the central information department sends out each year on a predetermined date videos of commercials from all over the world, organized by category. Maybe it's the best British, American, Japanese, or French campaigns. Or the best campaigns for alcohol, soft drinks, food, cars, and so on. Sometimes it's interesting. But it's rarely productive. When you see these films you are not in a position to make use of them. They are nothing more than of general interest.

Ideally, you should watch inspiring commercials at the moment you most need them. That is the moment when your homework is done, when your mind is in it and you're thinking about the best possible formulation of your disruption format. You are looking for complementary ideas or images, new associations of ideas.

This is why we created the Disruption World Bank. We wanted to provide planners with a tool that comes in handy at exactly the right point in their work process.

This Bank is a collection of five-minute video case histories showing and explaining strategic breakthroughs from around the world. Today, the Bank contains more than a hundred cases. A new series is added each quarter. While tools such as these are considerable investments, developing tools that encourage the association of ideas creates invaluable assets for any company. Each of our offices worldwide has its own Disruption World Bank system. This increases the odds of creating disruptions for all of our clients.

Each case history, whether it's from BDDP or another agency, is told through the eyes of Disruption. That is to say that each case traces the convention and/or vision that led to a disruption and describes the disruption itself and the results of the campaign. The software was designed to reflect the Disruption approach to strategy. In other words, the video case history database is classified according to the type of convention, disruption, or vision it represents. Not only does the software facilitate the association of seemingly unrelated ideas, it also serves as a pedagogical tool that reinforces the Disruption mind-set.

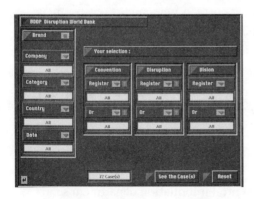

Say you're a planner, and you are looking for both a convention in consumer behavior and a disruption based on a tangible idea. You combine these two requests, adding a third concerning vision. You click the mouse three times and out of the bank's database of case histories appear the half dozen that fulfill your criteria. After watching them all, it would be hard to believe that at least one of them didn't inspire you with something new. You'll most likely broaden your perception of the problem, enrich the brief you're going to write, or refine your advertising proposition. This is the moment when the planner lets his imagination run wild. The Bank acts as a catalyst. It opens new doors for the planner, hints at new angles. Because the planner intuitively knows what he is looking for, the Disruption World Bank can help to find it.

The What-If Process

In addition to the Disruption World Bank, we have another tool—the *What-If Process*. We've all experienced being in meetings where everyone seems at a loss for new ideas. Then a question is asked and an idea suddenly comes to someone. Those questions always seem to fall out of the sky, like a simple and commonsense inquiry. If only we could know these questions in advance. We racked our brains and tried to remember the most provocative questions or interpretations which, at a given moment, sparked something. The ones that we knew helped us at least once to create a great campaign. Then we made a list of them.

We have come up with 60 questions that range from very strategic to executional. We have translated the list into a multimedia system that enables the viewer not only to read the questions asked, but to see examples of campaigns from all over the world that have been inspired by asking these questions. Here again, our objective is to increase our chances of making associations. A planner faced with an immediate problem reviews these 60 questions and, if one starts him or her thinking or takes on a particular resonance, then progress has been made.

Let's look at two examples from the list. Question number two is: What if we differentiate source of business from competition? One of the corresponding examples is the Printemps department store. Printemps's competitor is the Galeries Lafayette. They're located across the street from each other. You almost can't visit one without going to the other. Printemps's competitor is Galeries Lafayette, but its source of business is all Parisian shops. The goal is tapping business from this source, which is larger than the competition.

This new perspective of the market led to the store's revamping. Twenty years ago, it transformed itself into a set of shops that include the Boutique Blanche, Primavera, the Boutique Noire, the Rue de la Mode, and so on. This is an example that explains the distinction that can be made between business source and competition. While in most markets this differentiation is ineffective, if and when it is an apt one, the simple act of asking the question about business source will undoubtedly help you make progress.

Question number two is a strategic one. Let's move downstream in the list to an executional question. Question 46 asks: What if we reverse the logic of things? Heinz in Great Britain reverses the logic for its salad dressing by saying "Salads were made for it." The 30-second commercial boils down to a close-up of the sauce running slowly over the leaves of lettuce. A lot of appetite appeal. It gives the impression that the veins of the lettuce leaves were created expressly to highlight the sauce's creaminess and not the other way around.

Thinking about reversing roles can generate many ideas, especially when it comes to exploiting the parent-child relationship. A Danone campaign in Spain whose theme is "Learn from our children" actually shows children feeding their parents creamy Danone yogurt. Another Spanish commercial parallels this approach by making kids the ones who show their parents how to use a condom and who defend the practice of safe sex. Didn't Bob Dylan tell us "I was so much older then, I'm younger than that now"?

Logic inversion is an executional idea. Asking oneself about one's source of business is a strategic issue. The What-If Process purposely combines strategic and executional-type questions. Strategy by no means dominates. What counts is the catalyst that will help enhance the brief. Analyzing a campaign, like the one for Heinz or Danone, elicits a question such as: What if we reversed the logic of things? The What-If Process contains a wide range of questions, for example: What if a brand owns the benefit usually associated with another category? What if we replace a product reason-why by a brand reason to believe in the product? What if we deliberately choose a generic strategy? What if we show the effect of the product's absence? The question is always more general than the example that inspired it. So the question is what serves as a springboard for new thoughts, whereas the examples ensure the understanding of the concept itself. The goal of the What-If Process is for a question to inspire, to provide a relevant new departure point for the subject at hand.

Asking Better Questions

We want to be an agency that asks better questions than its competitors. One who asks insightful questions is a better listener. We are great believers in *creative listening*. And that is why we developed the What-If Process. The better the question, the more accurate the answer. In the Disruption methodology, searching for conventions is a questioning process. It is about not settling for the first answers that come to mind. It's about being suspicious of the obvious.

To anyone with a sincere desire to question and then challenge the responses, I recommend buying the Creative Whack Pack. This is a pack of cards listing 52 phrases that help topple conventions. Here are some examples: "See the big picture," "Think like a kid," "Listen to your dreams," "Get rid of excuses," "Don't fall in love with ideas," "Imagine how others would do it," "Dig deeper," "Imagine you're the idea". The Whack Pack is, in its own way, a What-If Process.

The Disruption World Bank and the What-If Process are the two tools we use the most. There is a tinkering aspect about them. I mean *tinkering* in the positive sense of the word; that is, in the sense that *tinker* opposes *engineer*. Tinkers use the means at their disposal. They gather and hoard things, saying to themselves, "This might come in handy some day." There comes a time when a Cadillac print ad, a Heinz TV commercial, or a Printemps poster triggers a reaction.

The Disruption tools enable us to navigate through a sea of data. Today, it is not so much having information as having the ability to find one's way within it that counts. The Disruption World Bank and the What-If Process are living tools. They're continually updated and enhanced. They are flexible. They serve as the heart of our shared body of knowledge. Everyone's tinkering and everyone's navigating contributes to them. Wherever it is, each agency in our network, through its culture, its own experiences, and the profile of its planners, must add examples to those that are generally available. The Milan and Amsterdam offices should gradually establish their own banks and their own what-ifs. Examples chosen collectively become references. By dint of referring to, discussing, and associating the same examples, office coworkers end up creating a shared culture. Modes of thinking ripen. People understand each other without having to spell out anything. The references people create together help them do the spadework on the issues even faster.

We want these tools to be a means for our agencies to enrich themselves and each other. A new experience creates a new case history, which in turns strengthens the tool. Every time a discovery is made, the collective memory is enriched.

Linear vs. Nonlinear

The typical advertising work process is sequential: overall company objectives, marketing strategy, advertising strategy, creative idea, executional format, and so on. This step-by-step linear process resembles an assembly line. You leave one point and move on to the next. The client's brief comes in at the beginning of the line. It's like raw material. The final product comes out at the other end.

Although this process seems practical, it is oversimplistic. It may help you order your thoughts but it can also rob you of some great sources of inspiration that arise during the final stages of your thinking. A purely executional idea that would normally be relegated to the end of the process can itself be the source of a new strategy or a new vision. In actual practice, then, we cannot allow linear logic to preclude the interplay of these concepts.

In the same way, the three stages of Disruption are not always sequential. As we've already stressed, thinking in terms of disruption is not a step-by-step process that you should always tackle in the same sequence. The three stages (convention/disruption/vision) can be approached in any order, depending on the subject or the inspiration of the moment. That's why we illustrate this relationship through a circle:

Articulating Thoughts

I even would go as far as to say that what counts is not so much filling in the Disruption format from the start as it is being able to fill it in at the end. Usually, the Disruption format will help you find the idea. But not always. If the idea comes from somewhere else, at the end of the day, whether it's precampaign or postcampaign, you need to be able to write a Disruption format in a coherent manner. Call it "retrofitting" if you like. Nonetheless, the Disruption format provides a way of articulating your thoughts. It's the report of your journey. More than a postrationalization, it's a way of verifying that you've truly created a rupture that serves a vision. In other words, contrary to popular belief, there's no harm in articulating the strategy after having found the idea.

You can rewrite, polish, fine-tune the format after the campaign is completed. There is no reason why downstream expression can't influence upstream thought. The thick wall that separates strategy from execution has to be torn down.

The Algorithm of Disruption

The Disruption methodology actually works a little bit like an algorithm. You enter the process at any point you wish. Then you complete the dif-

ferent steps, digging as deeply as you can into each one, and when you
have the feeling you've exhausted the subject, you go on to the next. You
continue this way until you come back to the beginning. Until a new association of ideas comes to light, you continue the process, enriching each
new time around with excursions into the Disruption World Bank and the
What-If Process.

Only a method that is flexible and open-ended can be inspiring. Yet because agencies' research departments are the ones responsible for creating
strategic tools, these tools are, more often than not, very conventional.
Structurally "too" perfect, constricting, and rigid in their logic, re-
searchers have trouble dealing with the diversity of real life, and with the
multiplicity of ways of thinking. Most often, the examples they use are an-
noyingly dull, which is not very encouraging. These tools are limiting
frameworks, designed to produce "correct briefs." And "correct" usually
means inert.

Disruption, on the other hand, strives to be open. It is not a laboratory
instrument but the sum of many experiments. It takes the best parts of us
and makes them available to everyone; it is strengthened by each person's
experience. You can enter it as you like, at the stage you want, at the moment you want. As we've just seen, you can even leave it aside and use it
at the end, as a method of verification. As a means of analyzing and sum-
marizing what you've accomplished. The Disruption methodology is not a
formula, it's a thought progression.

The Disruption Interval

In practice, when we start to work on a subject, we try to resist the obvious, get rid of assumptions, create hypotheses, look at situations differently, ask "What if?" and "Why not?" In other words, the objective is to
get out of the box.

Then we keep in mind the following: Never seize upon the first idea
that simply contradicts the convention. (We've seen that the opposite of
the convention is rarely the best idea; the answer most often lies elsewhere.) Be systematic in the search for disruptive ideas. Use the inspira-

tional tools of the What-If Process and the Disruption Bank. And finally, encapsulate the thinking in very precise wording.

All this thinking occurs between the marketing strategy and the creative process. Proposing mental strength to TAG Heuer, recognizing that Oil of Olay can stand for beauty at any age, suggesting that Nike should encourage us to surpass ourselves, finding inspiration in "The Penalty of Leadership"—all these ideas occurred ahead of the creation. Hence, the concept of the *Disruption Interval*. It is the interval between the client's brief to the agency and the agency's brief to the creative people. Agencies need to invest heavily in that interval. Some have forgotten that. They short-circuit this step without realizing that their clients expect them to invest in it.

Usually this interval is too short. There is not enough time. Something always has to be on air "yesterday." You're always one step behind the production deadline. Yet, the agency manager must find a way to confront these time constraints. His role is to optimize the time available. To constantly anticipate, to get teams thinking the very first day, and to never lose a minute. It's a daily struggle. The agency has to be organized in such a way as to guarantee that a maximum amount of time is devoted to the interval, to avoid a hasty leap from client brief to creative brief.

The Disruption Interval is an in-between time. This magical moment belongs to everyone in the agency. Everyone can make a contribution. It does not matter who comes up with the idea; the idea does not care. In this sense, we are all creatives.

It's the time when the strategic spark must be struck. A lot hangs in the balance during this crucial moment. The agency's life force, particularly the planners, have to think up tangible ideas, uncover consumer insights, or suggest new advertising registers. And propose them up front. To do this they need talent, intuition, and imagination—and, as I've said, time. The time spent in the interval is what ensures better briefs and, most often, better campaigns. It is also when the agency's culture is enriched and our body of knowledge increased. This is our own R&D.

Strategic Creativity

It is often said that strategy is the stage of analysis, relevance, and thoroughness, and that creative ideas have no place there. I don't agree.

Twenty-five years ago, when I was an account executive, I asked my boss what was the most important part of my job. Without hesitating, he answered, "The creative brief. Better briefs make more money." He added, "Think of the creative department as a factory." (I know some creatives who would not enjoy this analogy.) The faster the factory works, the better the company's productivity will be.

A lousy brief will have to be redone. A bad brief means time lost. A typical agency can lose a full third of creation time due to irrelevant or uninspiring briefs. Meanwhile, the factory is not running, and productivity decreases. A good creative brief, on the other hand, increases the probability of a great campaign. If a campaign is truly outstanding, it will last a long time. Less time will have to be spent on the creative work in the years to come. Less time spent means higher productivity and better financial results for the client and the agency.

We will always make more money by writing good briefs than by trying to save on office space and personnel expenses. One doesn't necessarily preclude the other, but what's certain is that there is a direct link between the quality of the brief and the bottom line.

All that we've said up until now and all that Disruption strives for boils down to one thing: A creative brief should not only be relevant, it should be inspiring. It must contain an *idea*.

Many would find this assertion shocking. For them, you have the strategy, and then you have the creative work. The two worlds are completely different. Totally separate. Therefore, talking about a creative strategy is irrelevant. It's nonsense. Worse, it's harmful. For them, a strategy is immaculate, untouchable. Its integrity must not be tampered with. It must not be affected by anything downstream. For them, the notion that an execution might affect strategy is dangerous. Anything downstream is trivial.

What's different about Disruption is that it requires that there be an idea in the brief, that the brief itself is creative. "Organic experience" is an idea for Clairol. "The power of the mind" is a thought for TAG Heuer. Ideas and thoughts are the seeds of inspiring briefs. They set the creative process in motion, encourage new ways of thinking, and often simply open up a new perspective, a new viewpoint.

It's easy to get caught up in hundreds of criteria for judging creative work in process. Yet you know instinctively if the brief is strong, if it contains an idea. In that case, there are only two questions that need to be asked. This first is: Could the campaign I'm watching have been created without the brief? If the answer is yes, the odds are that the campaign is lacking in content. You have to be able to see the brief in the campaign. The second question is a mirror image of the first. It is asked from the opposite perspective: Is the campaign merely a transcription of the brief? If the answer is yes, then there has been no creative leap, and the campaign lacks executional force. The brief should be in the work, but the work should not be the brief.

Creative Energy

Too often, a brief's lack of precision and imagination means that creatives spend several days, even several weeks, trying to sort it all out. Their energy is thus wasted upstream instead of being devoted exclusively to coming up with the best advertisement possible. Spending hours trying to figure out what to say is exhausting. So when creatives have to do this and must then start looking for campaign ideas, they're already tired of the subject. They have lost their freshness. And their drive. Thus, the issue of creative energy is critical. For creative people, the good thing about Disruption is that it lets them devote 100 percent of their energy to finding creative ideas.

Disruption also allows the creative director to raise the standards. If the brief is inspiring, part of the work is already done. This makes the creative director's job easier: He can push his creatives even further. And at the finish line, this is often what separates the good from the great.

We refer to all of this as the *creativity* of the strategy, as the idea in the brief. But it's easier said than done. The temptation to accept, or even write, an okay brief is strong. We must not give in. We must be demanding, insatiable. And make no concessions. We should be swept away by the beauty of a brief just as we are by the beauty of a campaign.

The Role of Planning in the Disruption Process

The planner's classic role is to know everything about the times we live in and about his target consumer. As François Dalle, the Chairman of L'Oreal, puts it, the planner must catch what is barely beginning. To accomplish this, he must be incurably curious, cultivate a sensitivity to the day and age, know how to listen, pay attention, and stay on the lookout.

The planner has to understand the target audience better than anyone else in the agency. His role is to interpret everything that concerns the brand. This requires knowing the right and most pertinent questions to ask and breathing life into often inert data. He or she must also understand how advertising works—that people don't just passively absorb messages, they react. What counts is what the consumer is made to think. The planner's role thus becomes ever more subtle: to understand how to make advertising interact effectively with the public.

This role, as it is classically defined, is essential. No agency can function without a strategic planning department that is knowledgeable and incisive. But planning should go even further. Planners must be creative in their own right. Most would judge planners on the rigor of their analyses and on the pertinence of their work. Planning also should be about encouraging difference. People usually value relevance; we encourage discrepancy.

> **"Disruption broadens the planner's role upstream and downstream."**

Disruption broadens the planner's role, upstream and downstream. Upstream, it's the planner's job to imagine brighter futures for brands. Downstream, it's up to the planner to generate the ideas that will help the creative people be even more creative.

Everything lies in the combined talents of planners and creatives. The most creative agencies in the world have the most brilliant planning departments. And planning serves no purpose in an agency without creative acumen. The creative team's imagination must exploit the planner's work to its fullest. The more precise the weapon, the more skilled the person using it must be.

Foundation Meetings

Because people know that a campaign can never be created by a group sitting around a table, brainstorming gets bad press in most agencies. They confuse the goal of brainstorming, that of coming up with ideas in the general sense, with that of finding ideas for an advertising campaign. Obviously, developing a campaign requires a special expertise. It's a technique of perfecting a message in a limited time or in a limited space.

Brainstorming, however, can be very useful for finding ideas upstream from the brief. The earlier brainstorming occurs in the process, the more productive it will be. We have instituted what we refer to as *foundation meetings*. These meetings unite not only the account people and the planners in charge of the budget, but individuals from other areas and at all levels as well. In our discussions, we don't set up a barrier between the upstream and the downstream. All ideas are welcome, be they strategic thoughts or executional ideas. Everything that is put on the table serves as the raw material for the planners.

Foundation meetings are effective for several reasons. Because they're held upstream, everyone's contribution is taken into account right from the start. They take place at a moment when everyone is relaxed, when no decision has to be made. At a moment when ideas can flow freely. When you're two days before any presentation, minds are more rigid. This can only obstruct the imagination. Moreover, by tearing down barriers, by mixing creatives with marketing people, by addressing upstream and downstream ideas, foundation meetings avoid falling into a linear process. There is no assembly line in the idea factory.

Foundation meetings can be more directly aimed at the study of conventions. They serve as opportunities to examine conventions both internally and with clients. We often have *convention sessions* with clients because they can identify better than anyone market and industry conventional practices. When involved from the beginning, clients are more inclined to accept the disruptive solutions proposed later on. We no longer seek to sell our campaigns but rather to give our clients the desire to buy them.

When you brainstorm in a convention session, you know what you're looking for; you have a goal in mind. At sea, when you are caught in a storm, you can quickly lose your way. That's why De Bono prefers the expression "brain sailing" to brainstorming. So do we.

Intuition

Whether we're thinking about conventions, visions, or disruptions, whether we're working our way through the Disruption Bank or the What-If Process, whether we're looking for tangible ideas or consumer insights, we can't do anything well unless we make room for intuition.

An advertising campaign is a solution to a problem. And that solution is rarely the fruit of step-by-step reasoning. At a given moment, the solution—that is, the campaign—imposes itself. You have not come up with the solution by deduction, you have made a leap. Leaps can be guided only by intuition. When you don't know how to get to where you're going, let your intuition guide you.

Two writers, Parikh and Jagdish, recently published a book, *Intuition, The New Frontier of Management*, filled with evocative statements. They presented a surprising distinction. For them, *analytical thinking* is a "northern" skill. That is to say, it is more a quality of Hamburg than Bavaria, it is more Scottish than English, more likely to come from Milan than from Naples. By contrast, *intuitive thinking* is a characteristic of people of the south; it is more Irish than Scottish, more African than European, and, they add, "more humanist than rationalist."

Because conventional, analytical, and logical thought no longer deal adequately with the world's growing complexity, they believe that "southern-type" thinking is going to prevail. That means that we should not hesitate to rely more heavily on intuition. For as a German, someone—probably from the south—once said, "Nothing intelligent has ever come from intelligence alone, and nothing reasonable has ever come from reason alone."

Daniel Richard, the CEO of 3 Suisses, which we've already discussed, was born in Nîmes, France. In other words, he's a southerner. For him, it's important to bring in sensitivity and emotion in order to give meaning to what you do. "That's why," he says "the role of a merchant today goes beyond selling products." For him, many big businesses have not yet understood this. Richard has transferred this belief to 3 Suisses' advertising. He explains that the 3 Suisses' territory is more right-brain than that of his competitors. He adds, "It's a soft, poetic territory because we place greater importance on feelings."

A cat always lands on its feet. One of 3 Suisses' ads shows a cat falling. It reads: "After the era of technology, statistics, surveys, grayness, marketing, reason, and prudence, here comes the era of intuition." Intuition has been 3 Suisses' theme for the past four years. Some ads sing the praises of intuition and tell people that there is no talent without it, or that art is intuition incarnate, and so on. Others talk about intuition in a less lofty way. For instance, one ad shows someone who has let herself be guided by her imagination. She has used Coke cans as rollers to set her hair. After all, she explains, "Things are always happy to come in handy more than once."

So, why sing the praises of intuition? In the business world—including in ad agencies—individuals are conditioned not to let their intuition speak. Ideas are acceptable only if they're based on irrefutable logic. Intuition is put down. This makes people undaring. They censor themselves. Yet according to biologists the part of the mind concerned with logic is located on the brain's surface, whereas intuition is hidden within its deepest folds. Therefore, giving intuition a voice is not superficial. On the contrary, it's the best way to express the sum of one's diverse experiences. That's why I constantly look for those sparks, those little telling phrases, that escape in the course of conversations. We don't know where they come from, but we can ricochet off them. Bill Bernbach used to say, "Knowledge is ultimately available to everyone. Only true intuition, jumping from knowledge to an idea, is yours and yours alone."

Overthinking

Analyzing convention. Searching for a disruption. Choosing a vision. The What-If Process. The Disruption World Bank. We will discuss sources of Disruption in the next chapter. Suggesting tangible ideas. Discovering consumer insights. Moving up and down the Advertising Ladder. What a mouthful! It's true that the Disruption methodology looks complex. But, in fact, it's not.

First, the expected result of Disruption is a single-minded advertising proposition one sentence long. Any creative director should refuse any brief that contains an advertising proposition of more than one simple statement. Less is more.

But that's not all. We should not confuse *simple* with *simplistic*. We know that for Asians simplicity is the ultimate sophistication. That also holds true for certain Europeans. Isn't that so for the English who see simplicity as the other side of complexity? Something simple is often proof that it's well developed. It should be clear that confronting the future always requires thinking. And especially that Disruption enables us to come up with strategies and briefs that are more deeply felt, more intuitive, more open.

There must be a period of time between the client brief and the creative brief. Otherwise the latter might turn out flat. You have to toss around ideas, come up with hypotheses, start to see solutions, and use the raw material provided by other people's thoughts. It's the planner's job to delve into the complex and to make it simple.

Disruption is not about making things complicated. Nor is it an exclusively rational concept, as some may fear. On the contrary, it's a method whose objective is to release feelings, intuitions, and emotions. It's a down-to-earth method whose objective is to help us think with our rational brains and our emotional hearts.

Disruption Methodology

Effortless

Finding a powerful proposition requires mastery and talent. But also, dumb as it may sound, it requires good old hard work. If we want our campaigns to look effortless, as though they flowed forth all by themselves, imposing themselves by their simplicity and their obviousness, we have to spend time working on them, thinking and using all the tools that enable us to find new associations of ideas.

Some evening when you're watching television, study the commercials. You can tell when ads are trying too hard. Their intentions are too obvious. They impose themselves without speaking to you. By contrast, there are some that grab your attention with their executional brio, but their lack of relevance is such that after you've seen them they leave you kind of empty. Great advertising combines the density of the content with the elegance of the form.

Disruption strives to achieve precisely this. But for it to bear its fruit, one's use of it must be thorough. It takes a lot of effort for effort not to show. The late Gene Kelly put it perfectly, "If it looks as if you've been working very hard, it's because you haven't been working hard enough."

8

DISRUPTION SOURCES

WE HAVE SEEN that Disruption, as a methodology, is based on three steps: convention, disruption, and vision. A convention is overturned, through a disruption, within the framework of a clear and well-defined long-term vision. We can pretty much imagine how to discern a convention or how to conceive a vision. But what about disruptions? What form do they take? How are they expressed?

The answer is simple: Sources of disruption lie at the crossroads where three groups—advertisers (companies), consumers, and agencies—converge. Each group corresponds to a disruption source.

The world of marketing is anchored in the concrete. It corresponds to disruptions based on *tangible ideas*. The world of the consumer is one of attitudes and behaviors. This is the realm where disruptions are based on *consumer insights*. Finally, the world of agencies is where advertising messages are generated, messages that can communicate on a number of different registers. In this sphere, disruptions stem from *advertising registers*.

All three sources are equally inspiring. It's helpful to examine them in more detail. In the following pages, we will explore at random, as though wandering through a video bazaar, the ideas to which they have given birth. This reflects the tinkering side of Disruption: Any idea, major or minor, as long as it is new, merits our attention and is capable of enriching our tools.

Tangible Ideas

Too many campaigns are forgotten the minute they are aired. The messages we hear and see have grown exponentially. Consumers are bombarded with hundreds of commercial messages a day. Faced with this message inundation, this oversaturation, the concrete can take hold. The mind can immediately hang onto something. The memory finds something to lean on.

We remember much more easily all that is tangible, concrete. And the fact that we are entering a world that is becoming more virtual, more intangible, doesn't change that. On the contrary, it makes it all the more true.

Tangible ideas are not advertising ideas per se, they are finds that are concrete and that make the brand proposition stronger. They can be many things. For example, a name that can in one fell swoop do half the work for you such as Night Repair or SnackWells. Or a packaging idea— L'Eggs pantyhose's egg-shaped containers, for instance. Night Repair and L'Eggs are each in its own domain clear-cut discontinuities. We will explore others in the following paragraphs.

The most interesting thing about tangible ideas is that they can also come from the advertising world. Take Chevy's, a chain of Mexican restaurants in California that airs commercials on the same day they are produced. Each spot begins with the headline "Fresh TV," thus driving home Chevy's commitment to the freshness of its food. "Fresh TV" is a tangible idea. Creating a 30-minute video and then using a 30-second commercial to sell the video is another example. That's what we recommended to Club Med, because it's impossible to convey in 30 seconds what the Club Med experience is and everything that it has to offer. When you take only one or two weeks of vacation a year, you can't afford to make a mistake. After all, nothing is more serious than the purchase of a week's vacation.

A 30-minute video for Club Med or 30 seconds of freshness for Chevy's are strong, tangible ideas. They are instructive examples to which we often refer. Tangible ideas like these usually come from an agency. Each one of them is not, in the strict sense of the word a "marketing" idea (although some can be elements of a marketing mix), and it is not yet an advertising message. They're *"pre-"* ideas. *Pre*campaign, *pre*message. They're ideas that are situated "upstream" from the campaign, before the construction of an advertising message. Their concreteness gives the commercials an incomparable impact.

We have organized tangible ideas into four areas: branding ideas, added-service ideas, event ideas, and media ideas.

Branding Ideas

If strong, in just one or two words the brand name can say everything about a company's positioning.

The Good Guys! is a California-based electronics retailer whose name becomes the force behind its advertising. Each commercial follows a mystery shopper into various Good Guys! stores. The shopper makes all sorts of requests of unsuspecting salespeople. In one spot he and his wife, who pretends to be pregnant, explain that they're on their way to the hospital. They need to buy a video camera but worry about the time it will take to apply for credit. "Instant credit" then flashes on the screen. In other commercials, our mystery shopper offers tangi- 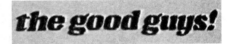 ble evidence of the truth of the store's name. From its low-price guarantee, its free installation in any location, and its promise that The Good Guys! never sell the wrong thing, each commercial is a service torture test, executed in a hilarious way. The campaign demonstrates the truth of the commitment of The Good Guys! sales staff: Everything boils down to action, not words.

The most interesting thing about this company, of course, and what determines the rest, is their name. You need a healthy dose of audacity and a bit of nonchalance to choose such a name. You instantly commit yourself. You guarantee dedication, honesty, warmth. The Good Guys! implies a friendly, service-oriented company that offers a nonthreatening shopping experience.

That's a great branding idea.

The very choice of the brand name saves a lot of time. Take, for example, the brand policies of Procter & Gamble or Estée Lauder, and the evocative power of brand names such as Pampers, Tide, Cascade, and Ivory on the one hand, and Turnaround Cream, Evanescence, Extremely Gentle Eye Makeup Remover, and Moisture-on-Call on the other. These companies exploit connotative names to their maximum.

Let's look at some other examples, such as Fruitopia and Little Caesars.

Lemon Berry Intuition, Mind Over Mango, Banana Vanilla Rupture, Love and Hope Lemonade, Peaceable Peach, Tangerine Wavelength, the Grape Beyond. The names of Fruitopia's flavors tantalize the taste buds and delight the spirit. The New Age has invaded fruit-drink labels. A flavor is no longer simply a variety with a plain name, such as orange, lemon, or raspberry. Fruitopia gives fruit a little wit and is instantly "with it."

There is nothing new in offering two products for the price of one. It's one of the most common types of sales promotions. But Little Caesars managed to make the mundane powerful. What the words "Pizza Pizza" initially reflected—a limited two-for-one offer—has become permanent. The tremendous recognition of "Pizza Pizza" encouraged Little Caesars to turn a tactic into the expression of its entire strategy: offering the best value. The magic of the mnemonic device elevated "Pizza Pizza" from a mere slogan to brand status.

The French word *nana* means "chick." It's also the name of teenage girls' favorite sanitary napkin brand. The packaging is so cool you can throw one in your bag without being embarrassed to open it. The name and the packaging are expressions of a relaxed attitude. No more affected modesty. You take a package of Nana out of your bag the way you would a tissue or lipstick.

Nana, like Fruitopia and Little Caesar's "Pizza, Pizza," was a disruption in its own right. A smart brand goes beyond a simple product name. The name itself can be an idea, all the stronger since it is by definition *tangible*. Pre-advertising the brand alone has gone half the distance. Disruptive brand names are tangible ideas that greatly enhance the effectiveness of the advertising. Even golf club makers have understood this point. With Big Bertha, War Bird, Heaven Seven, and Divine Nine, Callaway became a class in itself.

Added-Service Ideas

We can find an evocative brand name. We can also add a clever service idea that will highlight the difference between the brand and its competitors. Services that companies offer are often intangible—all the more reason for giving consumers something to grab on to. Darty, France's largest appliance retailer, has done this for over 20 years. Unlike its competitors, Darty never has sales or special offers. It was practicing the policy of "everyday low prices" before the phrase had even been coined. It created the Contract of Confidence, a pact between the company, its employees, and consumers, which outlined Darty's commitment to reasonable prices, carrying major brands, offering quality aftersales service, and so on. The Contract of Confidence is a real contract. It exists. It is concrete, and it is signed by each employee when he or she joins the company.

In this contract, Darty guarantees, among other things, repair on any day of the week (unheard of in a country where no one works on Sunday and where no stores are open). It's the tangible—the promise of Sunday repair service—that reinforces the credibility of all Darty's other intangible offers. There is a ricochet effect. Similarly, Leroy Merlin, France's leading do-it-yourself retail chain, promises to put you in touch with a specialized craftsperson to answer any question. Within five minutes of your first phone call. Guaranteed. Gitem, a group of midsize stereo stores, offers to repair your radio even if you didn't buy it from them. These are added-service ideas.

One of the best examples of making the most of added-service ideas is British Airways. And yet this has not always been British Airways' preoccupation. In fact, its efforts used to be concentrated solely on filling airplanes. Then British Airways realized that there was no way to compete other than to create new services, big or small. BA introduced the largest airplane seat, then arrival lounges, and even relaxation programs for the international traveler. Today, BA even offers showers in its lounges. Every initiative is part of a very directed and clear program of putting customers first. And when you really commit yourself to thinking about your client's needs there's nothing that's not feasible, even promising customers that all they need to do is turn up at the airport and they'll have a guaranteed seat to their destination. That's what BA's "Turn up and take off" program did. It simply promised that when a plane was full, BA would charter another one even for one customer. Unbelievable, but true. It's the idea of service at its maximum.

The art of using added-service ideas to distinguish commodity businesses is also an American specialty. What began as small corner copying centers have become the nation's first office centers for the virtual worker. Kinko's evolution and success has stemmed from simple service additions. When most people didn't have home or portable computers, Kinko's created computer workstations that could be rented by the hour, by the day, or by the week, complete with knowledgeable staff to come to any novice's rescue. On top of that, Kinko's made its services available 24 hours a day, 7 days a week. Kinko's has now added anything you can think of: faxes, desktop publishing software, express mail service, videoconferencing and conference rooms, and even courtesy phones for clients. Today, Kinko's is, as its advertising claims, "the nation's branch office," a complete office center for a new strain of American businesses.

Not a day goes by without a new initiative from Starbucks Coffee. Starbucks doesn't settle for serving coffee in 600 locations. It wants to turn its clients into coffee connoisseurs. Every Starbucks store goes beyond being a typical café; it is like a wine cellar of coffees from all around the globe. You educate yourself by letting your eyes wander. Starbucks has even gone so far as to publish a book series entitled *Starbucks Passion for Coffee* which is sold in all Barnes & Noble bookstores. It also produced a jazz compilation with Capitol Records, and then came out with a new kind of coffee called the Blue Note Blend. There's even a Nordstrom Blend. Starbucks is good at associating itself with cultural events and choosing the places where its coffee is served. Starbucks isn't just a roaster and a retailer. It is also the provider of all the ideas and services that elevate coffee tasting to a veritable art.

Jean-Claude Decaux manufactures and installs bus shelters in cities throughout the world: Paris, Madrid, London, Hamburg, Amsterdam, Gothenburg, Prague, San Francisco. Whenever Decaux goes abroad, it is faced with local competition. Winning over municipal councils requires a good fighting spirit. And, more important, good ideas. For example, Decaux has recently perfected a small device that beeps in your home when your bus is three minutes from your stop. Thus, you can catch your bus without waiting—a practical and safe solution. The latter consideration, security, is probably the one that will help it win the New York City market. An added service is a big added value.

Event Ideas

We've just talked about some of British Airways' added-service ideas that substantiate its claim as "The World's Favourite Airline." The list of its initiatives wouldn't be complete without mentioning BA's "The World's Biggest Offer," a one-day giveaway of every single seat on every single international flight. This event generated nearly $100 million of free publicity. More than a promotional idea, this offer was an event that could come only from a leader. Sixty million people applied. By carrying out all these concrete actions, of which "The World's Biggest Offer" was the crowning achievement, British Airways' claim as "The World's Favourite Airline" was imbued with meaning. It no longer sounded like a collection of vain and empty words.

For more than 25 years, the "Choice of a New Generation" has been Pepsi's theme. This campaign did not just appear full blown one day on the TV screen. It is in fact the fruit of the "Pepsi Challenge" and of all the taste tests that Pepsi has conducted for years, nationwide, against Coca-Cola. Nothing is more concrete than a side-by-side. And nothing is more powerful than a Pepsi Cola and Coca-Cola side by side. The roots of the "new-generation" campaign were very solid and tangible. The "Pepsi Challenge" gave the "Choice of a New Generation" its future mileage.

NutraSweet's launch was also based on a promotional idea that was taken up in advertising. The public's first taste of NutraSweet was in sampling NutraSweet gumballs distributed throughout the country in free-standing, large, old-fashioned-looking machines with the NutraSweet swirl logo prominently displayed. What better way to prove its good taste and positioning as an authentic alternative to sugar? The first ad campaign for NutraSweet then extolled the "first taste of a NutraSweet gumball." Today, over 3,000 products display the NutraSweet name and symbol.

Event ideas don't just have promotional roots, as for British Airways or Pepsi, they can often have PR ones as well. The WIN, or Wal-Mart Innovation Network, helps inventors, or anyone developing a new product, to find a manufacturer. More important, it provides the means for aspiring young inventors to translate their ideas into reality. When the fruits of these people's efforts become products, Wal-Mart distributes and markets them.

Casino, one of France's leading food distributors, was the first to exploit referendum marketing to its fullest potential. And as a result, some of its products were even forced to disappear from the shelves. It all started when Casino set out to create a panel of 10,000 expert customers. To recruit them, it launched an advertising campaign that called on all discriminating and difficult consumers to voice their opinions. By doing so, Casino committed itself to publishing any comment, good or bad. Here, the roles have been reversed. It's the advertising that becomes the tangible. The fact that Casino spends as much as it does on this effort is the proof of the seriousness of its initiative.

Dockers' "casual Fridays" is a great example of the potentially far-reaching effect of an innovative PR idea. It introduced "dress-down days" at a time when most American men's closets were filled either with work clothes (suits and blazers) or weekend clothes (jeans and sweats). Dockers' casual-apparel line was Levi's answer to an unmet need: casual, comfy clothes for baby boomers with a bit more cachet than jeans (and with room for the midlife paunch). The issue wasn't simply to get American men to buy Dockers, it was to get them to dress more casually more often. What better way to start a trend toward more casual work wear than encouraging avant-garde and often unconventional California companies to have dress-down Fridays? It was a simple PR campaign that sparked a national movement. Today, Americans have begun to dress more casually at work every day. Simplicity and comfort have become acceptable even in the most conservative industries. Now, more than 30 percent of American companies allow their employees to dress casually for the five-day workweek.

How would you do something different to introduce a new car series as the most advanced, state-of-the art driving experience? In South Africa, a car company did something completely unexpected and powerful, something that puzzled an entire country for more than a week. When a resident farmer alerted local authorities about inexplicable tracks that had appeared one morning in his field, the police were stumped as to their origin and concluded the marks may possibly have been made by a UFO. Such a preposterous assertion made such waves that the event was covered by the national news. But, in fact, the tracks were nothing but a PR initiative. Investigators in a helicopter discovered 10 days later that the mysterious tracks formed a 100-meter-wide BMW logo. The following day, the company placed full-page ads in all daily newspapers with the headline: "There is some intelligence out there. BMW." This seemingly crazy idea had the whole country smiling and was the first step in a great campaign for the launch of the Series 5 model.

Another car company that has successfully used an event to enhance its brand loyalty is Saturn. Its success has been anything but haphazard, particularly in the way it creates loyal and enthusiastic customers. For its biggest event since its inception, referred to as "The Saturn Homecoming," Saturn car owners were invited to the company's plants in Spring Hill, Tennessee. There were four days of festivities to celebrate the birthplace of their cars and meet the people responsible for making them. More than 70,000 people turned out—10 percent of all Saturn owners. Participants were spoiled with everything from plant visits to picnics complete with country-star entertainment to free paraphernalia to Camp Saturn for the kids. Not a bad metaphor for the company's philosophy of teamwork and commitment. And certainly not a bad investment of $5 million, or $70 per car owner, to reinforce the unique experience of driving a Saturn.

Event and PR ideas are tangibles. They bring force to the advertising message. They're often easily remembered. Five years postevent, both the Brits and South Africans remember, respectively, British Airways' "Worldwide Offer" and BMW's "There's some intelligence out there." Advertising simply served to highlight the event. In turn, the event is what made the impact of the advertising multiply tenfold.

Media Ideas

Brand ideas. Added-service ideas. Event and PR ideas. And last, but not least, media ideas.

Among the most productive tangible ideas are those that are directly linked to media. Take Nintendo, for example. It publishes a magazine through which Mario fans can learn tips on how to better play the game: to earn more lives, jump from one setting to another, and escape down secret passageways. It teaches them tricks to help them more quickly overcome sticky situations. People need the magazine to play the game, and, of course, they need the game to understand the magazine.

Another example of a *media idea* is to produce different types of commercials disguised as television shows in 60-second formats. Many have done advertising campaigns that actually have episodes, aired in a series. Sagas are created.

Even new channels are invented. For instance, Coors created its own TV channel. This tangible idea, called Coors Light TV, is a 60-second spot that acts like a condensed version of a regular TV channel. It is a series of 10-second clips of humorous beer-themed programs strung together whose effect is a coming attraction of a night of comedy television. These totally different programs are centered around beer, such as the sideways show where everything is shot from the perspective of a guy with a buzz, or the Coors' beach volleyball game, or even the Coors' play of the week. They offer an opportunity to communicate several brand benefits in one commercial in an unconventional way. For once, there is a television program that all beer drinkers will watch.

How would you get consumers to think about beer from the time they roll out of bed? Toohey's Export Beer in the United Kingdom created a takeoff on a morning news show. Complete with a male and female host, guest interviews, and on-location reporting, their programs became a new means of expressing the convivial atmosphere surrounding beer consumption. Some American brands have even gone as far as to use the infomercial format to disguise their own full-blown 30-minute television show. What better way to capture your target audience's attention if you're Sominex than creating the "Goodnight Show," which airs each night at 3 A.M.? Now even insomniacs have their own program.

Great media ideas are sometimes even exported worldwide. Taster's Choice borrowed the idea to create a soap opera–style love story between neighbors from its sister brand in the United Kingdom. It started when "he" borrowed "her" Taster's Choice. With *Dallas* no longer gracing the airwaves, Americans turned their attention to whether the neighborly romance would blossom. Local TV news shows even offered their own predictions.

MCI is another great example of creating disruption through a tangible idea. Its recent campaigns look much more like the coming attractions of a new TV sitcom or soap opera than like advertising. The "Gramercy Press" series, in fact, is all about a fictitious publishing company that, like some of its real counterparts in New York, is located near Gramercy Park. It becomes the metaphor through which MCI demonstrates the power of NetworkMCI, how it can help any traditional company make the  transition to modern technology. The first spot introduces the cast of characters and lays the groundwork for subsequent vignettes, each of which focuses on one of NetworkMCI's products. In the first commercial, the founder's son gathers his entire staff together to emphasize the need to replace the current tools the company clings to with more modern ones. During his speech, the camera focuses on the various staffers' reactions. At the end, Charlene, the office secretary, aware of the entire staff's bewilderment, turns to the camera as if we were part of the

Gramercy Press staff and says, "We'll talk." In each of the following vignettes, Charlene is cast as the narrator and the office champion of NetworkMCI.

In the electronic mail episode, we see the senior office employee in front of a blank computer screen. Obviously perplexed, he calls Charlene to find out if he has any messages. She tells him that he should look on his E-mail. He replies, "I want paper," then launches into a florid speech about how Dickens, Shakespeare, and Fitzgerald didn't use this stuff. Charlene simply replies, "Well, they would now."

There are dozens of commercials like these, all depicting the ups and downs of life at Gramercy Press. This campaign is really about making things tangible. MCI tries to make the implications of new technology more real for consumers. It shows that the digital age is not a vague fantasy of the distant future, but that it is happening right now.

Let's move north. Cossette, our associate agency in Canada, often underlines how abstract brands can be—that they can only come to life through different manifestations. Canada is home to more than a thousand brands of beer. Consequently, a beer cannot get recognition without a truly intrusive campaign. So, when it came to launching Molson Grand Nord, Cossette knew they had to create a campaign with unprecedented impact. The idea was simple: to create a huge media event that got viewers involved. Molson asked viewers to choose the endings of its commercials about the adventures of two heroes. The first commercial stopped before the end of the story. It proposed two different endings and had the country vote for the one it preferred. Surprisingly, 992,000 people voted. Fifteen percent of the entire population! The agency's anxiety was understandable when, two months later, it called for another vote to choose the end of the second commercial. Without the surprise effect of the first, everyone feared the number of voters would plummet. But there were over 1.1 million calls! It just goes to show that if you can offer something that gets people involved, they're ready to participate. Similarly, in France last year, a food brand asked television viewers to vote on whether to keep or change the campaign's sermonizing and imposing spokesperson. The French people decided not to make him disappear. They still wanted him to reprimand them for not putting enough of themselves into their cooking.

Weiden and Kennedy is an agency that seems to be strongly attached to tangible ideas. They're the ones who came up with the idea to launch Coke's latest product, OK Cola, targeted at Generation X, by creating a toll-free hotline. The number 1-800-I-FEEL-OK lets consumers react to the new drink and share their thoughts about feeling or not feeling OK. In addition, OK created a chain letter that encourages the feeling of "OK-ness" and asks recipients to keep the chain going by sending it to six friends. These two tangible ideas serve as the basis for OK's minimalistic TV campaign, simply text scrolled on a screen. The theme is the good fortune that comes to those who either drink OK or keep the chain letter going, as opposed to the misfortune that befalls nondrinkers and those who break the chain.

In one spot, an OK drinker inherits three houses, a yacht, and a fat cat from a man he doesn't know. In another, a girl who watches the TV chain letter later finds a crisp $100 bill in a parking lot. By contrast, those who choose to ignore OK get stuck in elevators for six hours and have to cut off their hair after stuff gets tangled in it. Each spot ends by urging viewers not to break the chain letter and by assuring us that "everything is going to be OK."

This might seem to be going too far. Outrageous at the very least. Nonetheless, what better way to incite trial than by creating a chain letter? So far, the toll-free number has attracted over 13 million calls from consumers.

I've always believed that fact-based advertising is more effective. But you don't always have facts at your fingertips. For lack of facts, you can create something factual. That is what's hiding behind the search for tangible ideas. People remember OK's chain letter, BMW's extraterrestrials, and MCI's Gramercy Park more clearly than they do conventional advertisements.

Underlying all of these examples is the will to make the intangible tangible. To make the invisible materialize. Let's look at one last example.

When you buy shares on the stock market, you rarely physically see them. Not very long ago we proposed that Cortal direct bank change that. We presented them with a recommendation entitled "What if Cortal made shares materialize?" The idea is to print, sell, and market tangible shares that you can buy and sell over the phone, but also file at home. A BMW share could be systematically offered to the buyer of a Series 5 model. The buyer would find it in his glove compartment. The Hermès share would doubtless be embellished with the lovely cloth ribbons that decorate the gift boxes of this most elegant worldwide boutique. Cortal makes stocks tangible consumer goods.

We have now looked at numerous tangible ideas, from The Good Guys! to Molson Grand Nord, from Nana to NutraSweet, from British Airways to Cortal. This may look like a motley bunch. Like a bazaar of ideas. But it is useful. It works as a library—an imaginary library. We love using these examples as references. They build up our collective memory.

We've seen that planners can no longer simply be people of data, but, rather, they must become sources of ideas. Edward de Bono's reminder that "analyzing data will not produce new ideas" certainly rings true when you think about the ideas for "Fresh TV," OK Cola's consumer chain letter, and Ben & Jerry's sponsorship initiatives, and that a planner could have been behind each one of them.

So, whenever we start to work on a new campaign, we force ourselves to ask these questions: Can we come up with a tangible idea? Can we launch "Fresh TV?" Can we create a Danone Health Institute? Can we create a Web or a television saga? Can we materialize what does not yet exist?

Consumer Insights

Effective, original, and inexpensive tangible ideas are not easy to come by. A second source of inspiration may be found in what we call *consumer insights*.

One jeweler says, "Show your wife you'd marry her again." An automobile manufacturer doubts that you would sell your present car to a friend. A drink with a strange name reminds us that "the first time is never the best." A cosmetic brand asks, "Does your husband look at you the way he looks at other women?"

Consumer insights are observations about life. They're a little like stolen moments, fleeting forays into real life, revelations of the way people think or what they do. If a particular manner of thinking, feeling, or acting has not yet been discovered or exploited by your competitors, you've got your chance. You may have the starting point for a very involving campaign. You see an ad that says, "What if you have reached that difficult time when you are older than your boss?" If that is the case, the ad immediately speaks to you. A consumer insight is an incursion into people's real lives. If an advertiser accurately portrays what you are feeling or thinking, you are already won over. We are always drawn toward those who understand what makes us tick.

Twenty years ago, motorists were fearless. Now they're more afraid behind the wheel of a car than on a seat in an airplane. Today, people no longer eat to live, they eat to be healthy, as long as that doesn't mean giving up too many things they like. These observations, these consumer insights are the things that reflect people's attitudes and behaviors. Consumer insights are not the same as consumer expectations. Any product can strive to fulfill a given expectation. But it is a consumer insight that gives life and depth to the message that highlights a given expectation. A woman wants to be beautiful at any age: That's the expectation. Women now talk openly about aging, even embrace their age: That's the consumer insight.

Consumer insights stem from people's ways of thinking, of doing things, and of feeling. They're observations about people's attitudes and behaviors. About those small habits that, in fact, make up the seeds of life.

Ways of Thinking

I have worked in three different agencies. Three times I have prospected for oil companies. Three times I began my presentation with street interviews of randomly selected people, all of whom displayed a complete lack of interest in gas stations. Even as they were pulling out of a station, some interviewees couldn't remember the brand of gasoline they had just pumped into their tank.

It's never been a positive experience for a company to find that the consumer thinks its products and services are generic. Yet, surprisingly, when Total, France's largest gas-station chain, put its account into review, it was not taken aback when all the agencies involved in the pitch confirmed this reality. They all conducted the same interviews and showed the same footage. And they came up with the same recommendations. Except for BBDO Paris, who proposed doing the unthinkable: airing a short cut of the footage as a 30-second ad on television and turning it into the commercial that would launch Total's next campaign. Six or seven people answer an off-camera interviewer's question:

"Sir, could you tell me why you chose this service station?"
"Purely by chance! I just stopped at the first one I saw."
"And you, ma'am?"
"Because it's a service station. Easy as that."
"And you, sir?"
"No particular reason."
"And you, ma'am?"
"That's easy, my car just broke down. Why, does it matter?"

The voice-over concludes: "There's nothing worse than indifference. At Total, we are doing everything possible to make sure that soon you will no longer choose us by chance."

This commercial was the foundation of the campaign. It was daring to air it on TV. Total accepted the idea that gas stations are all the same and dared to make a case of that fact. This commercial acted as a *reason to believe* for the campaign that followed. Everyone thought that if Total could air such an ad, it's because they were determined to do something. This was one big incentive, both externally and internally: Overnight, every Total employee felt bound to try harder.

Since then, Total has made bottle warmers, impeccably clean restrooms, and air pumps available in every station. They guarantee that the bucket of water you use to clean your windshield is changed every hour. They make filling your gas tank a less messy affair by providing gloves. And most important, they have created the Total Club Card, which provides customers with driver assistance and information services (itinerary planning, traffic jams, emergency messages). The card also offers the bearer, for a limited time and in exchange for a tank fill-up, guaranteed free road assistance for 15 days. Total has left nothing to chance.

What Total did was simply to put on screen what many consumers feel. By dramatizing a consumer insight, its advertising effectiveness increased tenfold.

Kirshenbaum & Bond is especially proud of its ability to create impact through what it calls "word-of-mouth" advertising, proof that television is not the only means to change consumers' ways of thinking. Take Citibank. One magazine ad shows the picture of a hand with a large engagement ring, and the baseline asks, "Was it for love or was it for the miles?" Another one depicts a fancy sports car: "Was it a midlife crisis or was it for the miles?" And a picture of people on a lunch date: "Did she take me to lunch to be nice or was it for the miles?" It's true that more and more people have joined in the quest for miles. It's become a pastime. That's why the campaign plays upon the tendency to treat mile-collecting as a game. It creates an inside joke with the consumer, who wonders, "What other sneaky things will people do to get miles?" And offers a new way to think about miles.

A typical middle-class New Yorker in shorts and undershirt is playing with his dog in the yard. We hear his wife, who has a heavy Brooklyn accent, call him in to dinner. We then realize her husband is in the middle of a manicured garden the size of a football stadium. When he does not immediately show up, his wife shouts out directions like a drill sergeant to guide him through the garden maze to what turns out to be a Tudor mansion. This is a New York Lottery commercial. Also memorable is the ad with the cheerful tollbooth collector who pays the tolls for every car and truck that passes through. And the teenage delinquent who "just bought an oil company last week." Building upon the previous "A dollar and a dream" campaign, the "Hey, you never know" campaign casts playing the lottery as a new form of entertainment. It encourages people to fantasize about what they would do if they won. Playing the lottery is no longer about winning, but rather about dreaming about winning. Very insightful.

Citibank, the New York Lottery, and Total are all about revealing a shared thought, a way the greatest number of people perceive things. When viewers share the belief exposed on screen, the brand easily wins them over.

Ways of Doing

Who hasn't bought a pair of jeans that doesn't fit? Who hasn't gotten annoyed trying them on? Each of Lee jeans' commercials reminds us of  our reality and captures the difficult experience of putting on a pair of jeans: A man turns soprano as he squeezes into a pair, a woman tries on her entire jeans collection giving her date the time to meet, fall in love with, and marry her roommate, and so on. Being the "brand that fits" gives them a bit of fire power to combat Levi's veritable institution. By illustrating the consumer's experience of the product, Lee carved out its own territory . And not without humor.

Have you ever had someone next to you on the bus or on the subway who is trying to read your paper? Have you ever been doing a crossword puzzle when someone rudely looks on and trys to offer advice? Have you ever been at the Laundromat and been told that the machine you've just put money in is already reserved for someone else?

The British Broadcasting Corporation used these analogies from everyday life experiences in its advertisng to help the British public understand what it is like if they do not pay their TV tax that gives them access to all public television: They're simply freeloaders. They took people's ways of doing and symbolically transferred them onto the screen. By illustrating poor behavior on screen and likening it to watching TV without paying the tax, the BBC woke consumers up. Today, tax revenues have increased threefold.

One small observation about a motherly habit in one country changed behaviors and consumption levels the world over. Take Vicks, an ointment for chills and minor colds. It is sold the world over. In Mexico, the quantity consumed is significantly higher than anywhere else. And yet it's not especially cold there. The explanation is simple. When a child has a cold, the mother rubs Vicks not only on the child's chest but also on the throat and back. She believes that the cold will be cured only if all three areas are treated. Procter & Gamble turned this habit into an advertising idea and exported it to the whole world. From then on, the theme of the campaign, from the Philippines to Germany, was the healing power of mom's hands and Vicks VapoRub for all kids' body parts that get into mischief.

The Lee, Vicks, and BBC campaigns do not reflect profound attitudes. They are simply observations about day-to-day life and the way people act. It is when we look around us that we make interesting discoveries. Inspiring ones.

Ways of Feeling

People can think and act in the same way. They can also have shared feelings.

In Spain, Sogo Fashion Stores even go as far as apologizing to women for reminding them that their common remedy for feeling low is to go out shopping for clothes. Sogo's entire campaign then exposes the causes of women's depression. Each commercial is based on a question such as: "Have you ever noticed that while you're constantly dieting, some women eat, eat, eat, eat, eat and never gain weight?" Then the voice-over adds, "We're sorry to remind you of this, but, when you're feeling depressed, you just go out and buy clothes." Sogo shows that shopping is the best way to lift women's spirits. Just think about how many things can make you depressed. Lots of things, lots of commercials, lots of questions such as: "Have you ever noticed that most men who are especially handsome are . . . gay?"

Perhaps one of the most widespread feelings is the fear and frustration that most people have in dealing with their respective banks. No one has expressed this better than a midsized regional bank in the southern United States, First National Bank of Commerce. Its advertising dared to demonstrate the reality of poor service in the banking industry at large and the advantages inherent in dealing with a smaller, more personal bank.

Shot in black and white from the perspective of a bank security camera, complete with a time counter in the corner of the screen, each spot in the campaign gives us an insider's view of life at a large bank. We see the back of an elderly man speaking to his banking representative. The customer says that his statements seem to have extra, rather expensive charges on them. The bank employee curtly responds that he should have asked for a cheaper account. Visibly vexed, the man asks, "You mean you've had a cheaper account all along?" The impassive banker replies, "I didn't know you wanted one." A black panel then flashes on the screen: "You have just witnessed a bank robbery."

In another spot, a bank employee informs a couple that their request for a loan has just been turned down. When the wife asks why, the employee gives her the stock answer, "I guess you weren't a good risk." The husband is shocked, given that they've been good customers for 10 years. As the employee explains that this was surely taken into consideration, she inadvertently reveals that she doesn't even know the couple's last name. A black panel tells us, "You have just witnessed a bank failure."

This time the camera focuses on a man sitting restlessly in a chair, waiting to be helped. Many bank employees pass by, and when he asks them for help, complaining that he has been there over 30 minutes, they ignore him. Suddenly, these words appear: "You have just witnessed a bank holdup."

We all know that, for banks, we are not customers. We are risks. Good risks or bad. And we are afraid of not being good ones. That is the most universal of consumer insights. No one expressed it better than First National.

Consumer insights are thus the second source of Disruption. It is the uncovering of the consumer's "unexpected truth" that creates involvement. In order to bring them to light, you have to be attentive, noticing the little things that make up everyday life. You have to look for these shared ways of thinking, doing, or feeling. You have to be observant, re-lentlessly tracking down the ways in which your contemporaries live. You have to adopt "a detective attitude."

Advertising Registers

You've tried to think of a tangible idea. You've come up empty. You've searched for a consumer insight. Nothing to exploit. A third source of in-spiration involves changing the register of expression. That is, creating a discontinuity in the way a brand expresses itself in advertising. Choosing a new angle, changing one's tune.

We have expanded the idea-territory-value grouping into one that de-fines six types of advertising expressions. This tool, which we refer to as the *ladder*, serves as the base from which we can identify each possible mode of expression.

> Top of Mind / Attribute / Benefit / Territory / Value / Role

One source of disruption can be found by asking oneself, *in which area on the above ladder would I like to situate the campaign?* You must choose. Do you want to reinforce top of mind awareness (like frogs croaking "Bud . . . Budweis . . . Budweiser")? Highlight an attribute (like Avis' "We are num-ber two")? Emphasize a benefit (like Tide's three-sock demonstration on cleanness)? Stake out a territory (the way Levi's sells a bit of America in Europe)? Reflect a value (the way Nike glorifies going beyond one's lim-its)? Or, finally, claim a role (like Virgin, which promotes youth culture)?

The objective is to shift the advertising focus from one advertising reg-ister to another in such a way that it creates a rupture in both content and style with what has gone before. Remember, it was Nike in the early 1980s that went from attribute advertising to value advertising. At a given mo-ment in a brand's life, moving from one register to the next on the ladder can be highly disruptive. Pepsi moved from a taste benefit to the new-generation territory. IBM abandoned its mainframe-oriented campaigns.

Saturn asserted deeply traditional American values. Virgin championed music's place in our lives. All these brands have chosen an angle. Each has an elocution of its own. They all have particular modes in which they express themselves. They've forged their own repertoire. They created a discontinuity in their copy history. They "disrupted."

The message's register of expression must be chosen "upstream." For some, this question might not seem to be of primary importance, but in fact it is essential. We believe it's a strategic, not a creative, decision. It therefore creates heated discussions. But ideas are born from confrontation.

Benefit

The most conventional way of writing an advertisement is to emphasize the merits of a brand by showing a benefit and, if possible, to illustrate the benefit on the screen. For many, this is an immutable law. Detergents get clothes white, cars are safe, drinks quench thirst, and insurance companies provide security. And it's even better if you can manage to say credibly that the result is whiter, safer, more thirst-quenching, or more secure.

Many people think that a benefit can't be anything but a promise. Yet a benefit can be the simple act of using the product. The pleasure of the *experience*.

French knitting wools have always vacillated between selling the product (wool) or the end result (the sweater). Phildar sold something else: the pleasure of knitting.

Experiencing a product can create a shock to the consumer. It can change his life. "I thought that Kama Sutra was a Portuguese monk until I discovered Smirnoff," said one ad. "I was the mainstay of the Public Library until I discovered Smirnoff," said another. "It was tea for two until we discovered Smirnoff," said a third. For the British, drinking Smirnoff is really an experience. This campaign in the late 1970s opened their eyes to the good things in life, and when it did, they understood even better the signature that told them "the effect is shattering."

In the United Kingdom as well, Tango orange drink saw an opportunity to celebrate its unique product effect—the citrus tang that hits you at the back of your throat on the first sip—by dramatizing the explosive aftertaste. This idea led to the creation of a series of zany commercials in which an orange monster slaps an innocent Tango drinker upon taking his

first swig from the can. It ends with the tag line, "You know when you've been tangoed." By coining the term "tangoed" and demonstrating the effect in a tangible, physical way, Tango is no longer seen by English consumers as just another soft drink. It's not just about quenching thirst, it's about the hit one gets from it.

Tango and Smirnoff sell us an experience. But they go even further, so that when you drink a glass of Smirnoff or Tango, the advertising images immediately come to mind. For them, advertising is part of the product experience. They know that people consume advertising as well as the brand.

Attribute

Ariel came out in 1968. It was the first detergent with enzymes, or, as they said at the time, the first "biological detergent." When the reason-why is factual and exclusive, the work is already done. Twenty-seven years later, Ariel is still the leader in France. By a long shot.

Such convincing reasons-why are not always at our disposal. When you lack one, it is then necessary to sift through the facts, in order to find something that is as tangible as a reason-why. Factual information always enhances a campaign, gives it a certain depth. Remember the spectacular Saatchi ad for British Airways inspired by *Close Encounters of the Third Kind?* A spaceship crosses the Atlantic. The vessel is none other than the island of Manhattan itself. Concrete information—British Airways carries more than two million people across the Atlantic every year—gave rise to one of the most famous commercials of the 1980s. You can't beat a fact.

A fact is not, strictly speaking, a reason-why. It's a reason to believe. When Avis claims "We try harder," you believe it, because it underlines the fact that Avis is number two. When Ivory tells us it's 99.44 percent pure, we believe it, because it thus admits it can't be 100 percent pure. When Crisco said, "All the oil comes back . . . except one tablespoon," it admitted that french fries do indeed absorb one tablespoon of oil. But only one.

Faced with facts, we give in. That is why campaigns based on attributes are often very effective. They give us reason to believe.

Territory

A territory is not a benefit. It's a mixture of form and substance. It makes the brand unique. We've already talked about the "Old Money/New England" style of Ralph Lauren. You find it in the product design but also in the point-of-sale material, and even in the choice of photographers such as Bruce Weber. By building a coherent identity for all the forms in which the brand "expresses" itself, you create a territory. Fashion designers and perfume producers excel at this.

But others do, too. As early as the 1970s, for example, Benson & Hedges created its very own territory. It was the first brand (along with Charles Jourdan shoes in France, photographed by the wildly imaginative Guy Bourdin) that dared to be surrealistic. Nothing is more commonly seen than a pack of cigarettes. Nothing is handled more visibly. And nobody wants to smoke the same brand as everyone else. Using a new register, one that contained echoes of Magritte and Dali, the brand landed in a league by itself. The campaign played up cultural elitism and lauded the strange. Later, Silk Cut in the United Kingdom decided to follow a similar path.

Nescafé is an instant-coffee brand. In France, it has built for itself a distinct territory by appropriating the imagery of the neighboring, referent category—coffee beans—as its own. The commercials are colorful, titillating minidocumentaries on the Andes. They show the Indians of the Altiplano, with native music in the background. This is truly a matter of appropriation. Nescafé abandoned the downstream, the conviviality of families enjoying a cup of coffee, in favor of the upstream, the exotic places where arabica is grown.

A territory can be imagery. But it can also be a trend. Ever since the Second World War, American products have been popular among young Europeans. Both Coca-Cola and Levi's have in their own way used the myth of American youth to their advantage. During the 1960s and 1970s there were the so-called lifestyle campaigns. Now executions are more original and varied. Yet they reflect that myths can remain contemporary.

We've seen that Rodier celebrates women of today. But when you think about it, you realize this campaign was not totally convention-free. It continued to portray women who like to be looked at. In the United States, Levi's for Women goes one step further: It conveys the way a woman sees herself. All masculine references disappear. In one of its commercials, a Matisse-like figure in clothes that are nondescript except for the blue pants is introduced by the title "Woman Finding Love." As in a moving painting, the woman floats from scene to scene with classical, melancholy background music that seems to guide her. When she comes across new figures, they are suddenly transformed into words written in black script: Lust, False Alarm, Loneliness, Luck. The blue lady finally lands on a heart, which then transforms itself into the Levi's for Women logo. I've shown this campaign to many people. Men are more or less indifferent to it. But women adore it.

Value

Shot from overhead in austere monochrome, the scene shows a heavily built skinhead running away from a car. We're told that "an event seen from one point of view gives one impression." The camera angle then changes to a sidelong perspective and you can see that the skinhead is ag-

gressively running toward an elderly man. The voice-over continues "seen from another point of view, it gives quite another impression." The skinhead lunges at the man. Then the camera angle switches to show that the skinhead is not assaulting the passerby. Instead, he is pushing him away from a pile of bricks that is about to fall on him. It concludes, "but it's only when you get the whole picture that you can fully understand what is going on." Then on a black screen appear the words, "The Guardian."

I like this commercial. It's one of my 10 all-time favorites. "The Guardian" illustrates how difficult it is to be a good journalist. To have a good perspective, you need to give yourself the necessary distance. "The Guardian" chose to stand for professionalism and objectivity. Its advertising expresses it brilliantly.

Classic FM, a British radio station, could simply have boasted its differences. Instead, its advertising advocated the feelings that music evokes: Power, exhilaration, and love. In other words, Classic FM decided to own the emotions that it brings to the public. Today, Classic FM is the most listened to commercial station in the UK.

Trying to represent a value can fit within the vision of a brand. Objectivity, emotion, confidence, progress, balance, outdoing oneself, and nostalgia are only some of the values that brands have stood for in recent campaigns. Let's look at what two leading French companies have done.

French trains are very fast. Last year they beat the world record by reaching the incredible speed of 300 miles an hour. In Europe, everyone takes the train, few people take the plane, and almost no one takes the Concorde. When you realize that in the past the train was the primary means of transport in Europe and that, due to the oversaturation of airspace and thanks to technology, the train will again become so in the next, the SNCF's slightly nineteenth-century-sounding theme, "Progress is only valuable if it is shared by everyone," is especially apropos.

In its country of origin, Evian promises balance. Not just the right balance of minerals it contains, but an overall balance of life. In other words, drinking Evian guarantees an improved equilibrium of mind and body. It gives you what no other water can. For Evian, the water we drink is as important as the air we breathe.

Embodied values can be more personal. Johnson & Johnson Baby Powder is the brand that best captures what is shared by a mother and her child, starting at birth. I remember one commercial that was a hymn to newborns. The voice-over said, "Johnson's Baby Powder would like to welcome your brand-new baby into this world and make it soft for him," over a very soft background melody. "Before he can see you or hear you, he can feel your touch. So use Johnson's Baby Powder. It's almost as soft as love." Perfect. Moving. Irresistible.

The value personified by a brand can change over time. Keds traditionally sold itself on practicality, solidity, and comfort. Then, not long ago, the brand took a sharp advertising turn. Keds are also soft and supple; they are very feminine shoes. The commercial is a series of images, a trip through time. In each stage of life, Keds are there. And the voice-over asks, "What size Keds were you wearing when they stopped delivering milk? When you got too big to be carried? When your mother was the prettiest woman on earth? What size Keds were you wearing when you learned to take a compliment? When you started to hold your father's hand again? What size Keds will you be wearing when the first of your friends gets married? When a woman walks on Mars?" Since 1916, American women have worn Keds at all stages of their lives. People who buy Keds own, on average, several pairs in various conditions in their closets at any given time. "Keds never stop growing," says the claim. Here we have authenticity, nostalgia, and femininity. Watching these commercials, women feel happy to be women. Keds offers its own vision of femininity and womanhood.

When you have a richly textured brand to work with, you mustn't hesitate to raise the level, to deepen the message. If you can, you must, as they say. If a brand has established a legitimacy that allows it to embody a value, that legitimacy must not be squandered. You must never under-leverage a brand.

Role

A brand can adopt a role. Leclerc is a chain of independent, midsize supermarkets. It has taken on the mission of removing the mental and legal blocks from French society. That's a big job. Specifically, Leclerc fights against everything that is an obstacle to competition. In France, Vitamin C can be sold only in pharmacies. "Vitamin C is not allowed to be sold in Leclerc stores. When will oranges be sold in pharmacies?" is their answer. In the same way, they attack the French bank monopoly when it comes to financial services, they sell gold jewelry at half the price of the retail standard, and they even go as far as to sue clothing manufacturers who refuse to consider them as a distribution outlet because, at Leclerc, the manufacturers can't sell their clothes at the prices they do elsewhere.

Leclerc already had the image of being the least expensive. With its campaign to overturn rigid rules of business, it reinforces that image. Everyone knows that lack of competition means higher prices.

Nothing is more important than having a home. That's why Maison Phénix, the leading house builder in France, promotes the idea that "every house should be a home." As for Condé Nast, it acts as the advocate of the written word by telling us that "the importance of technology will never be greater than the ideas it is meant to convey." Dockers even takes on the mission of "battling against rules, conventions, and any other 'forbiddens' that make life uncomfortable and boring for all men."

One of the best examples of role advertising comes from Spain. It features a dog whose young master is glued in front of the TV and has forgotten him. The dog opens his suitcase and places in it his bowl, his brush, and a photograph of the boy, closes the suitcase, picks it up between his jaws and, with a final glance at his zombielike master, sadly walks out the door. This commercial was a directing masterpiece and received the Grand Prix at Cannes. It was also a show of intelligence, for it was none other than the Spanish television channel TVE that had this commercial made. TVE claimed for itself the role of advising children to watch less television. When it comes to raising a discussion to new levels, TVE is exemplary.

When you're an analgesics producer, it may seem difficult to go beyond promising the best pain relief for such and such a symptom. Yet, UPSA Laboratories, one of the leading over-the-counter medicine producers in France, gave itself the role of better understanding pain. This battle reflects a very disruptive mission, one that no other analgesics producer has dared to take on. In its advertising, UPSA demonstrates the importance this role has at a very individual level. For example, one print ad shows a beautiful infant on one side and copy that reads "Pain. Matthieu, three months old, too small to talk about it, but big enough to feel it" on the other. Nobody likes to talk about pain. Everyone prefers to focus on the relief. By concentrating on pain, UPSA adopts the stance of a leader and gives itself an important and valid position in day-to-day life.

Things have changed since 1984, and in its more recent commercials for the PowerBook, Apple revamps its message in a way that is better adapted to the 1990s. In 1984, freedom was still an important issue, and the Macintosh message was modern in that it extolled humanity's liberation from the machine. Today, the issue at hand is individual freedom of expression and personal development. The PowerBook makes this new freedom possible. The implicit supporting argument is no longer the user-friendliness of the language but the flexibility of the PowerBook's use, its seemingly limitless adaptability, and the diversity of its applications. Today, liberation is not functional but intimate, sensitive, as the more

than 20 commercials of the campaign show. Apple's "What's on your PowerBook is you" campaign reflects its belief that the PowerBook can be as many things as there are individuals to shape it. Your PowerBook doesn't resemble any other. It's personal. It shows who you are better than anything.

Leclerc, TVE, and UPSA. All of these brands assigned themselves a role, thereby raising themselves a notch above the rest. Like Virgin, which we have already discussed. Its anthem that there is never enough room for culture in our lives is expressed in a commercial that borrows its style in many respects from Murnau and Fritz Lang.

The scene, shot in black and white, takes place many centuries ago. A man dressed in an ancient costume is voraciously eating pages from a book. The words "As the century draws to a close, cultural starvation sweeps the land" flash on the screen. We then see another eerie-looking character stirring a witch's caldron from which musical notes rise like steam. Then the rest of the culturally deprived and desolate population is shown gazing at a poster that states, "Nothing to see," while the tempo of

the music accelerates. The words "Enough is enough" appear while the angry horde stampedes forward and tears down the poster.

The sky starts to rumble and we see the title, "A goddess appears before famished hordes." An obese yet majestic woman wrapped in a white tunic descends from a mountaintop toward the stunned crowd. Marvelous chants accompany her magical gestures. The diva lifts her hands toward the sky and the words "Virgin Megastore" appear. The crowd pulls on a cord that turns a pulley, causing a cast-iron wheel containing the words "music," "books," "videos," "stereos," and "restaurants" to rotate. Finally the words "None will ever forget" flash and our goddess slowly draws away from her enlightened horde, returning to her temple on a distant mountaintop.

On the final screen, we can read the end of the story. "From that time forth, the cult of Virgin Megastore was perpetuated day after day from 10 A.M. to midnight in the great cities of the world. Virgin Megastore."

It's not enough to proclaim, "You can never make too much room for music." You have to have a certain amount of legitimacy. This commercial, and the posters that have appeared throughout the store's seven-year life, have helped Virgin claim the role naturally. The advertising style created the legitimacy.

Top of Mind

A giant thermometer, in which the mercury has been replaced with beer, reads 1664°. In a dance competition, four contestants turn to reveal the numbers on their backs: 1, 6, 6, and 4. A telephone has only buttons that read 1, 6, or 4. These are the unusual images that are juxtaposed in a baroque commercial aimed at increasing the awareness of Kronenbourg's premium beer, 1664. Too often, we forget that simply seeking notoriety can inspire powerful campaigns. And effective ones, too. Who could forget the frogs from the "Bud . . . Budweis . . . Budweis . . . er" ad?

We can simply create brand awareness. We can also try to dramatize the importance of the brand. Michelin does this perfectly when it says "Because so much is riding on your tires." So does Dunlop in the United Kingdom with an ad that expresses consumers' attachment to the brand when it says, "You'd be surprised how much you'd miss Dunlop." The commercial that illustrates this claim begins with a woman playing tennis. Her ball disappears as she throws it up for a serve. In a montage of scenes, a series of similar events befalls people as various Dunlop products vanish. These include tile adhesives, Wellington boots, wheels and tires, firefighting equipment, mattresses, and so on. It's unforgettable. But, more important, it highlights in a visual way how central Dunlop is in the life of the British. Demonstrating how much the presence (or the absence) of a brand matters is a way of acknowledging the brand's importance. It constitutes a register of expression that is often highly intrusive. In the Dunlop ad, no benefit is shown. It limits itself to building impact on presence or absence. That is why I file this approach under top of mind.

Obviously, top-of-mind campaigns are a little more down-to-earth than those based on values and roles. This results in the implicit sense of hierarchy on the ladder, with "top of mind" at the bottom and "role" at the top. Yet I fight against this idea every day. No single register is necessarily more effective than the others. Knowing where to place a brand on the ladder is a strategic decision. The ladder casts light on the possibilities. It helps you imagine a multitude of different ways for a brand to express itself.

Brand New

At a given time in its life, a brand changes the content of its message. A tangible idea is conceived that reinforces what it communicates. A consumer insight is discovered, giving the brand more resonance. Or an advertising register is changed, thus creating a discontinuity in the brand's copy history.

The brand decides to "speak" differently. It questions itself. At first, we are caught off guard. The Guardian and Levi's commercials, the ads for Leclerc, Benson & Hedges, and Keds, all took people by surprise. These brands lead us to see them in a different light. It's their new voice that gives them a second wind. They are rediscovered. They are brand new.

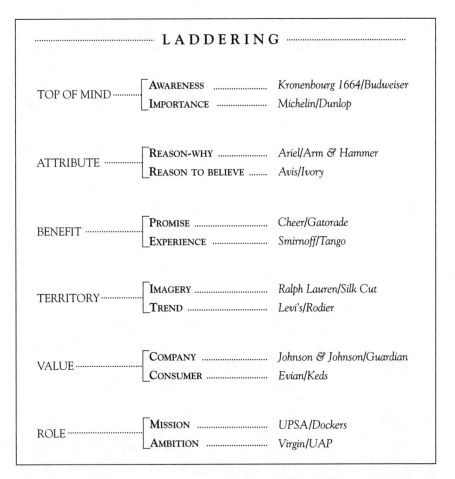

LADDERING

TOP OF MIND	AWARENESS	Kronenbourg 1664/Budweiser
	IMPORTANCE	Michelin/Dunlop
ATTRIBUTE	REASON-WHY	Ariel/Arm & Hammer
	REASON TO BELIEVE	Avis/Ivory
BENEFIT	PROMISE	Cheer/Gatorade
	EXPERIENCE	Smirnoff/Tango
TERRITORY	IMAGERY	Ralph Lauren/Silk Cut
	TREND	Levi's/Rodier
VALUE	COMPANY	Johnson & Johnson/Guardian
	CONSUMER	Evian/Keds
ROLE	MISSION	UPSA/Dockers
	AMBITION	Virgin/UAP

Laddering is a great way to give a brand's advertising new possibilities. This chart is my personal example. It's helpful to come up with your own, one that is relevant to your country's culture and your own personal taste.

PART IV

DISRUPTION AND
THE ROAD AHEAD

If you don't change to respond to the times, you obviously become vulnerable. Like all other domains, advertising can survive only if it reinvents itself, if it anticipates the future by disrupting the present. To move forward, agencies currently face two challenges. The first one is located downstream: coming to grips with the technological revolution. This is the subject of the next chapter, "Disruption in the Information Age." The other is upstream: reclaiming the agency's legitimacy as a strategic adviser. This is argued in the final chapter, "Disruption and the Role of the Agency."

9

DISRUPTION IN THE INFORMATION AGE

AS THE FINAL lines of this book were being written, the navigational software, Netscape, had been public for six months. Its listing was unprecedented: a capitalization that went as high as $4 billion for a company with less than $80 million in sales, whose primary activity during the first quarter of 1996 consisted in giving away free software. Netscape's visionary and disruptive initiatives are just one indication of the radical implications of new technology for business at large. Even Microsoft has been forced to make sweeping changes in its strategy.

Netscape's revolutionary software is one of many things we thought were impossible that are suddenly being done. For the last five years, we have been deluged with articles and books that hail the coming of the information society. We can pretty much imagine this new society's contour. But only the outline. Visualizing a concrete image of things and understanding all that the superdigitalization of reality implies is no easy task. Hypotheses fly and interpretations abound. Yet, while nothing is unimaginable anymore, there is only one certainty: We are all going to become experts in constant conversion.

Multimedia does not simply weave together new communication channels that complement the existing ones. It is creating entirely new ways of thinking. The world will belong to "digital kids," that generation with no memory of life before MTV and personal computers and that doesn't even know which company—Apple or IBM—is older. More important, after years of interfacing with computers and exposure to thought patterns that branch out, the very way in which digital kids' brains work will be different. They will think less in a traditional, linear, narrative way, and more in a treelike fashion. Their ideas will be linked but not strictly linear. This generation's thought processes will be different not just in degree but in nature. There will be a discontinuity.

Ad agencies are gradually coming to grips with this new reality and what it means for their interaction with the consumer. They recognize that multimedia not only signals a time for change, but offers a springboard for them to enter new domains of activity, to take on new roles, and to shape new ways of communication. For instance, they are slowly getting used to the idea of leaving behind the term as well as the very idea of a target. From now on they know that this group (which we have the annoying habit of referring to as such) will be able to talk back. They know full well that consumers will be able to choose not to listen to them. They understand that if they want to get through to consumers they have to invent new languages and new ways of talking. Dialogues, not monologues.

Interactivity and Creativity

While the information superhighway may not yet be paved, the Internet is a good harbinger of what is to follow. So are the cable networks' current experiments throughout the world. Interaction with the audience carries with it endless possibilities for development, whether it's providing direct access to subjects the public is interested in or producing made-to-order programs. Digital television, which will allow each of us to become the editor of our own news program according to our own interests, is on its way.

Because each viewer will be an editor, capable of concocting his own television programming, the notion of having hundreds of channels doesn't make much sense anymore. It is this imminent shift from *broadcast* to *narrowcast* that will give the advertiser total consumer *addressability*, much more than the 500 channels we're told are on their way. With narrowcast, consumers will finally become clients. While it will have taken digitalization 20 years to help make Lester Wunderman's oldest dream come true, advertisers will at last be able to establish an ongoing dialogue with consumers. This new one-to-one dialogue can be formatted as follows:

Convention	Advertisers see their target audience as passive consumers of messages.
Disruption	The new media enable consumers to develop individual, active relationships with brands.
Vision	From now on it will be through these one-on-one relationships that brand loyalty is created.

We already know that modern technology has accelerated the pace of competition and that creating loyal consumers has become the most critical stake in the game. What will count is not only overall market share, but also what percentage a brand has of each individual's total purchase. In other words, the percentage of Oil of Olay, for example, that each consumer buys will be as revealing as Olay's overall market share.

Because consumer-share strategy will be first and foremost a strategy of loyalty, brands must take advantage of every chance they get to make contact with customers in order to get to know them better. Yet, are they doing this now? No. Each day, most brands miss any number of such opportunities. How many database files, for example, are being left empty when time lost means giving the competition a powerful weapon? How many consumer brands have implemented a real consumer-loyalty program within the core of their heavy users? How many advertisers still don't realize that they should consider the media not as suppliers but as partners with whom they share the same consumers—those consumers whom they know on a case-by-case basis? Building relationships with consumers is a detailed, meticulous, and ongoing process.

Modern technology means power for the consumer. His ability to zap and even avoid traditional advertising has increased tenfold. Interactivity is gradually putting television viewers in the place of readers who can select, buy, flip through, pick up, and put down their books and newspapers as they wish. It is in these types of media that advertising can impose itself the least on its intended audience. All of this is hardly a secret, yet many people continue to act as though tomorrow's advertising will still take the form of tried and true direct mail, updated to fit the norms of the age.

We know that it takes more than mere adaptation of old advertising techniques applied to new technology to come out ahead. It means that we are going to have to invent new languages and to redefine what we mean by "quality" advertising. Interactive media users will choose the ads they like, when they like. They will even be able to pay not to see them. But because they will want to watch their Sunday night movie free of charge, they will voluntarily inflict 10 minutes of commercials on themselves. Because consumers will no longer approach advertising passively, now more than ever, we are going to have to get them to buy not just the product, but the advertising itself. This calls for more creativity. From now on, only apt, intelligent, appealing, or funny images that speak to them and say something new will be worthy in their eyes.

To keep consumers' desire aroused and to encourage their loyalty, brands will have to constantly pique their curiosity. This will mean exploiting the participatory aspect of modern technology to its fullest. Agencies will have to understand what companies like America Online have known for a long time: The role of multimedia will be to deepen relationships on an individual level. Only involvement counts. The reason for America Online's success where pioneers like Prodigy have failed is simple: America Online understood the primacy of *relationship value*. Users want to get together, to have a sense of camaraderie, of community, of clan spirit.

It was with this same goal in mind that we created a cyberclan for Clan Campbell Scotch whiskey. Today, Campbell consumers have become individuals with a shared obsession: December 31, 1999. The Clan Campbell Internet site is the vehicle through which consumers are transformed into clan members. By encouraging their participation "real time" in the first grand initiation game on-line, what was once simply a shared enjoyment of a Scotch brand has become a shared interest. At the heart of this virtual treasure hunt is the quest for acceptance into the clan. This site hooks consumers into a game that, over the course of the next three years, will take them from being candidates to initiates and, finally, selected members of the clan. It is only by immersing themselves in the treasure hunt that allows them to partake of the mysteries and secrets of the lands of the clan. Those who have solved the puzzle and gotten through the traps of the game become elected members of the clan. What's great about this program is that it transforms a Scotch whiskey from a product into a collective experience. Its members will be invited to meet their fellow clanspeople at an incredible bash that's very real, in a Scottish château, where a huge party will herald the third millennium on December 31, 1999.

The "Unique Unifying Proposition"

More than ever before, content will prevail over form. Multimedia is not an end in itself. It is a means to an end. It simply opens up new communication opportunities that complement the major existing media. Multimedia is only a partial substitute for what already exists.

One thing, however, is sure: The interdependence of media venues will multiply. Given their proliferation, no single medium alone will be able to touch enough of the people enough of the time. None will offer enough reach and frequency. The cumulative effect of an advertisement will come only from multiplying one's chances of being seen in a wide variety of media.

An advertising message will therefore have to be transversal, transmissible in a wide variety of forms. Above all, it will have to be strong enough to become anchored in people's minds, powerful enough to unify the inevitable disparities in execution and broadcast venues. Its force will have to counterbalance media's fragmentation. With the shift from unicity to multiplicity, the 30-second commercial will no longer do all the work single-handedly. While that doesn't imply the end of the unique selling point or the good old selling idea, it does mean that its role will change, slide a bit. Until now, the selling proposition guided the conception of a 30-second television commercial. It guaranteed the ad would be linear and simple. In a word, it ensured single-mindedness.

Now, new media venues require that the idea, or more simply, the message unify. The idea must enable the use of new modes of expression, of new executions that differ greatly from one medium to the next. The role of the next generation of USPs will be providing a strong link between diverse executions. Unique Unifying Propositions will connect the dots. They will unify, while simultaneously allowing multiplicity.

There was something deliberately simplistic about the selling idea. The brand's message was distilled into a specific, limited promise, such as "Good to the last drop." Obviously, a commercial, a poster, and a CD-ROM can't and don't convey their respective messages in the same way. Consequently, future themes will have to be broader, more open, and will unify the overall brand message. They will be in the vein of "Just do it," "The choice of a new generation . . . ," and "Success is a mind game." The breadth and depth of these messages invites a plethora of diverse executions and at the same time *unifies* the brand's message.

TAG Heuer is a case in point. Its theme, "Success is a mind game," has given birth to executions that run the gamut from breathtaking commercials and evocative and esoteric print ads to concrete initiatives that bring the notion of mind over matter to each individual. Tag's creation of a CD-ROM enables anyone interested in sports to gain access to interviews with a number of champion athletes—interviews in which they talk about how they push themselves mentally to accomplish great feats, how they psych themselves up just before the gun, how imagination spawns motivation. The new information technology provides a way for everyone to better understand the champion mentality and bring it into their own lives. After watching these interviews, people won't look at TAG Heuer the same way anymore. The interviews add depth to the message. The theme reconciles the horizontal discourse of conventional media with the vertical discourse of the new. This change can be outlined as follows:

Convention	An effective message is one that is single-minded.
Disruption	The new media are opening up an era of multiminded communication.
Vision	Effectiveness will become a matter of integrating a multiplicity of messages into a unique unifying proposal.

New media bring everything to a personal, individual level. Thus, they can no longer play the role of "general alert," a function which is necessary to create a powerful impact on the public at large. The more accessible the information, the more people will need points of view and opinions to get their bearings and make sense of it all. There will be an increased need for brands to leave a clear and precise imprint, something for consumers to grab on to—all the more reason for agencies to be intimately involved in defining what it is that consumers can grab and the *unifying message* that will help them find their way through.

Agencies in the Digital Age

Because content and its vehicle are becoming inseparable, agencies are in a privileged position to oversee the marriage of the two. Thus, multimedia's constant blossoming presents agencies with a skyrocketing number of opportunities. All they have to do is seize them and avoid the temptation to view new technology as simply "new media." Agencies occupy a unique place—in between the advertiser, its client, and the digital kid, the new consumer. They must act as the interface between the two and create languages that will be truly user-friendly in the literal sense of the word.

With the proliferation of TV venues comes not just an increased fragmentation of advertising messages, but of TV program viewership as well. In order to increase their chances of being seen, these programs will have to be tailored to fit the desires of their audiences. I'm willing to bet that, just as it does for consumer products, the agency will give its opinion on the offer—even to help in its design. On one side there's Hollywood, and on the other there are the cable operators. And in between are the agencies who, better than anyone else, can help these two worlds communicate, knowing that they have little reason to understand each other. New technologies will spawn a new form of bartering, one that will continue to grow. From the conception to launch of any product and anytime two disparate groups need to be brought together, agencies have a role to play.

All of this simply means an overwhelming number of challenges. That the future is a blank page on which the advertising business has many lines to write.

DISRUPTION AND THE ROAD AHEAD

This can be formatted as follows:

Convention   Agencies create ads.
Disruption   An agency's role is to facilitate communication between disparate groups of people.
Vision   Agencies must construct languages.

Michel Troiano of Ogilvy Interactive believes that "the winner will be a shop that is part ad agency, part software designer, part client service organization, and part publisher. . . ." Many agencies are redeploying themselves in accordance with this horizontal mode. A few of the things we do in Paris are indicative of this trend. We developed the software that monitors McDonald's sales in real time. We publish, on average, 3.5 general public magazines the size of *Newsweek* per week. We create food educational programs for 70 percent of all the nurseries in France. We hold sales-training programs for trade marketers. We build loyalty programs for car dealers and bank customers. We imagine all possible scenarios and

make crisis simulations in cases of nuclear accidents. We advise state-owned companies how to manage their institutional relationships when they privatize. Because the spectrum of our clients' expectations expands each day, we have to continually rise to meet the challenge.

We have developed CD-ROMs for a number of clients, such as Chase Manhattan, TAG Heuer, and Pringles. For France Telecom, we produced the first advertising campaign on the Internet in France. We designed the Virgin Megaweb, the Virgin Megastore's Web server, the first electronic magazine in French (and English) with such quality of editorial content that

the trade press hastened to compare it to *Hotwired,* the American gold standard of sites. It is currently one of the most frequently accessed sites in France, ranked third at the end of 1995. In addition, we got our clients involved in the CD-ROM distributed by the market's leading monthly magazine, *CD Media*. 3 Suisses, for example, used it to present excerpts from the Virtual Exhibition they sponsored.

But most important, we are venturing further and further into the world of interactivity. We have spent months digitalizing our legacy of print and television ads so that they might be preserved and thus accessible on demand. We recently inaugurated our very own site, called *Disruptif*, which, among other things, gives a weekly hit parade of top Web sites—in other words, the most disruptive ones. The Disruption World Bank, which contains information in text, audio, and video form on about 100 case histories of advertising disruptions, was available on videodisc long before the invention of CD-ROMs. Soon, I hope, we will have our own *Intraweb*, the company's in-house Internet server, which will be a living storehouse of any and all useful information. These data will no longer be buried underground in the archives but will circulate freely through the computer network. Vertical archives will make way for an accessible storage system. Everyone will be able to get to whatever information he or she needs whenever he or she wishes.

Why mention all of this? When the future is hard to predict, you have to experiment, learn by doing, and gradually visualize what's opening up before you. Fiction meets reality—a fictive reality. The virtual is the cause and the effect of interactivity. Interactivity is the root of the proliferation of communication channels. It draws concentric circles that we enter and exit at will. All this we know, but what we don't know yet is how quickly it will affect our daily lives. It's up to advertising people to be on the lookout, to keep their eyes and ears open, to anticipate.

Agencies have to play a close game. They have to be more and more shrewd. Because interactivity generates dialogue, it demands of advertising people a great deal of discipline and excellent listening skills. True work on themselves. Before interactivity even existed, we used to say, "The important thing is not what is said but what he or she who sees our message is led to think." From now on, the public will react once and for all. People will thus become active players in advertising. They will decide whether or not to play the game.

10

DISRUPTION AND THE
ROLE OF THE AGENCY

THE 1980S WERE a decade of excess in all its forms, in advertising as much as anything else.

It was a time when some people confused cause and effect and thought that advertising was powerful enough to have been the ultimate cause of the demise of the state-controlled economies of the socialist world. According to Peter Sealey, former marketing and advertising head of Coca-Cola, advertising played a significant part in bringing down the Berlin Wall. It is his belief that "little 30-second commercials of kids drinking Coca-Cola, eating Big Macs, listening to a Sony Walkman, or just doing it in their Nikes brought a dream to enough men and women, boys and girls, to change the world." He continued, "And it was not just the brands that were shown in these ads. It was the laughter, the smiles, the vibrancy of life they portrayed that got to them. The totalitarian, dogmatic, dull, gray, lifeless, planned society could not withstand the relentless pressure of advertising." A free market as a condition precedent to a free society . . . and advertising as a lubricant for a market economy.

It was a time when advertising people were interviewed on the evening news at the drop of a hat and asked to share their views on the important events of the day. A time when the least little agency was listed on the stock exchange. A time when in London there were more than 20 listings in three years, and when the big advertising agencies such as Saatchi & Saatchi capitalized their earnings more than 25 times. Money was raised with a snap of the fingers. I know what I'm talking about, because I remember how one simple phone call once freed up the extra $20 million needed to close a deal in the United States. It was a time when the Saatchi brothers were thinking about taking over Midland Bank.

The time of extravagance and immoderation has been scaled back to size. Although probably for the best in some domains, especially in advertising, the backlash was excessive. Today, the advertising business has been knocked off its pedestal. Agencies have let the pendulum swing back too far. They have scaled down excessively. They have added salt to their economic wounds by accepting drastically reduced fees, which has in turn aggravated their predicament. Worse, agencies have stopped investing. What ever happened to the wonderful training programs that Ogilvy always used to organize? Who still cares enough about investing in the future generations?

The bottom line is that the advertising industry of the 1990s is suffering from a brain drain and a dilution of talents. These are not my words but those of Mike Cleary, vice president of advertising for Procter & Gamble Europe. Very few companies place as much importance on advertising as Procter & Gamble, for whom success is derived from a combination of great research and development and good agencies who communicate its products' competitive edges. For P&G, the two are inseparable: They regard "superior product performance and insightful premium advertising as equal top priorities in the long-term success of their business." P&G even calls its marketing branch "the advertising department." Well, Cleary has a rather grim view of things. For him, "we are no longer attracting the best and the brightest. We are a people industry and we don't invest enough in people."

The Mike Clearys of this world aren't alone. A few years ago, Roger Enrico of Pepsi asked, "Why should great marketing minds go and work for an advertising agency?" The answer was in the question. He didn't see what agencies really brought to the party as far as marketing was concerned. A study published in 1993 by the Louis Harris firm is even more discouraging. When asked, "Where do you think change will come from in the future?", 56 percent of those asked predicted R&D and 40 percent said corporate planning. Advertising agencies were named first among all outside advisers but attained only 8 percent.

For me, the future of our profession hinges on our ability to shift those percentages, to reinvest in ourselves to remedy Cleary's ominous vision and to answer Roger Enrico's unsettling, yet telling, question.

Renaissance

The reality still remains that advertising agencies have a special position. They're suppliers and partners. They're both in-house and independent. They're the one outside adviser with such a deep knowledge and understanding of brands and of what's at stake for their companies that they can provide their clients with fresh perspectives. And, because the agency lies at the crossroads of many different domains and activities, the mental agility that it brings to the party, coupled with its inherent distance, is unparalleled. Ries & Trout refer to advertising agencies as the "perennial outsiders." This is more than a truth; it's all advertising agencies' raison d'être, the one key asset they need to exploit to its fullest to progress.

I would summarize the way we must view ourselves as follows:

Convention	Advertising is losing its influence.
Disruption	No other outside adviser is as close to clients.
Vision	Agencies are consultants. Consultants with imagination.

Agencies must rid themselves of the conventions that hinder them and reclaim their legitimacy as strategic advisers. It is true that agencies have lost ground in this area. Their stature has eroded. Yet nothing could be more natural for an advertising agency than to act as a consultant not just for advertising but for all of its clients' business issues. The logic behind this belief is crystal clear: If you want to produce the most effective advertising execution, you need the most inspiring strategy, which in turn requires a thorough knowledge and understanding of the brand, as well as a clear idea of the brands' area of expertise, its possibilities for successful line extensions. Pondering diversification boils down to asking ourselves,

"What business is this brand in?" or, if we want to be faithful to our concept of vision, "What does this brand stand for?" All those questions require going back upstream from the execution, to the brand strategy, and often to the corporate strategy.

We can get there only by proving that we know what is dearest to our clients' hearts and that we understand the public as nobody else does. In other words, it's up to agency people to establish legitimacy. To make themselves irreplaceable partners in the creation of brand and company visions. To reestablish themselves as consultants. But not just any kind of consultants. The consultants with imagination. It is only this condition that can spark a renaissance. We will then avoid getting stuck in a peripheral role.

Our goal should be to show Roger Enrico that marketing people, too, can be inspired by agencies. That they can benefit from our work on a diverse set of problems in disparate industries. Immersing oneself in one field after another, from banking to yogurt, from cars to medicine, is stimulating. An agency is a melting pot of marketing experience. Its ability to ricochet ideas from one domain to the next and apply its acquired knowledge, coupled with its savoir faire, to any situation constitutes its reason for being. And that it is precisely what makes agencies irreplaceable.

James Young, the founder of Young & Rubicam, used to say: "I propose to assume that if a man or a woman is at all fascinated by advertising it is probably because he or she is among the reconstructors of the world." If I were to adapt Young's optimistic statement to today, I would say that it is up to us to make our clients fascinated by advertising again and to make them see the power of advertising to help them reconstruct new worlds.

The Structure of the Future

Verticality is a thing of the past. People don't generate ideas simply by talking to their bosses. The horizontal inspires. Transversality authorizes discontinuities.

Ideas have free reign only when boundaries no longer exist. When someone says, "I am speaking as a specialist of such and such discipline or as a representative of such and such institution," he betrays a refusal to think. In information technology, as in all fields of modern science, progress is made thanks to interdisciplinarity and the coming together of a variety of skills.

Anyone in advertising takes this transversality, this horizontality, for granted, for this way of working is inherent to all agencies. Yet it is Charles Handy who reminds us that this is in fact one of our most precious assets. In his latest book, *Empty Raincoat,* he explains that businesspeople should "look at an advertising agency for an approximate model of how we shall be working tomorrow. An advertising agency arranges its people in clusters . . . of expertise. The creatives or the planners or the people who book the space in the media. They are drawn from these clusters into a range of account groups where they work on the requirements of a particular client or product. They may work on several different account groups, and the membership of the group will flex with the demands of the work. It is a fluid matrix organization." A little further on he adds, "Their members have a tightly specified core, but space for initiative and improvement, often a great deal of space."

When companies such as IBM, AT&T, BT, and Xerox "deconstruct," or reorganize themselves into networks of autonomous units, it is true that, structurally speaking, they are not so far from an advertising agency. While decompartmentalizing and squashing hierarchies can be a very difficult and delicate exercise, it is the very transversality they strive to create (in other words, the combination of the expertise and creativity of one discipline with those of another) that makes true advances possible.

Horizontality is not about words but actions. For a group effort to be truly productive, no one discipline can override another. This is all the more difficult in that every company, because of its own internal culture, which itself is the offspring of its history, often favors one field in particular, whether it's sales, finance, production, or marketing. In an agency, no one discipline is more noble than another. Each with its own area of expertise, contributes on equal footing. No group dominates. Thus, when the group is faced with a problem, it does not feel the pressure of an official or implied hierarchy either. This is how companies whose survival is dependent on the creativity of its employees should be organized. Imagination is a fragile thing.

Speed Is Power

We've mentioned several times "Fresh TV," Chevy's campaign that airs commercials the very day they are shot. While today "Fresh TV" is the exception, it won't be for long. The latest technology is going to break down barriers, throw off deadweight. Soon only hours will separate the conception and the airing of an idea. Messages will undergo constant renewal, modification, and improvement. We'll have to get them on air as quickly as possible. Speed will be an end in itself.

Paradoxically, the more time technology helps us save, the less time we have. Things and ideas expire before they are completely used up. We are experiencing a pandemic acceleration. Flexible structures such as advertising agencies, software companies, and cutting-edge consulting firms possess a mobility that makes them more equipped to rise to this challenge. With the fusion of data and data processing, power lies in lightning speed—in the rapidity with which we can access and digest data in real time, to manage them instantly. In a word, the power to annihilate downtime. It's a tough challenge. But one to which agencies must rise if they are to survive. In one of his latest works, *L'Art du Moteur*, the intuitive and original philosopher Paul Virilio writes, "Information derives its worth only from the speed with which it is delivered. Speed is information itself!"

Networking

At the turn of the century, fewer than 50 percent of professionals worked for a company. The others were simply independent. In the 1980s, 90 percent of all professionals were company employees. A few years from now, at the beginning of the next century, we will probably see a return to the 50 percent. Who says this mass tendency was natural? It is surely more natural to belong to smaller groups or to belong to nothing at all. Today, all companies must be open to outside expertise. As Tom Peters says, "It's arrogant to believe that the best person to get the job done is in your building."

Here, too, agencies provide a glimpse of the shape of organizations of the future. They have no problem with networking because they are networks themselves. The trick is knowing how to make the most of having offices throughout the globe. A network is not just a bunch of flags printed on the same map. It is the sum of a variety of skills and expertise. The network's management must highlight and stimulate them. Assigning to every urgent and challenging problem an ad hoc, multinational, and pluridisciplinary team is one of the most thrilling tasks I know of. It's a mind opener.

If you build up a network based in New York, it will ultimately "think American." This is not a problem. Of all the money spent on advertising in the world, 50 percent of it is spent on American soil; 70 percent of global brands are of American origin. If you build up a network based in Paris and you start to "think French," you're as good as dead. Your only chance consists of creating a genuine multicultural network. You have to cultivate deep roots in each of the countries in which you operate. Know which cultural buttons to press to sell more. Identify where the specific talents hidden in each of your agencies lie. Cultural diversity also means avoiding fixed and generalized solutions. Never impose a worldview, be it American or French (or even English . . . which is, of course, better than both).

Cultural diversity is not just about mixing nationalities. It's about bringing people from diverse areas of expertise and business cultures together. An agency, like any "living" business, has to be accustomed to working with outside sources. I'm not talking about the usual freelancers, but something on a much higher level. I'm referring to leading thinkers, experts in specific domains. Take Claude Fischler, a member of the CNRS (the National Center for Scientific Research) and one of France's greatest nutritionists. He has greatly enriched BDDP's ideas for "Danone Active Health." Emmanuel Todd is one of the most well known demographers in France and the world. Thanks to his help we were able to sharpen our ideas for a very big French distributor. While we know how to hire external talent, we don't necessarily know how to make the most of it. To en-rich our multicultural diversity and to exploit it to its fullest potential we have put together a permanent board of 10 external consultants. The board is actually on the agency's payroll. It acts as a part-time—or rather, shared-time—consultant, exclusive to us.

Thus, partly by chance and partly by deliberately keeping an eye on what's going on around them, agencies represent in their organization ex-emplary structures in many aspects. Such an assertion will surely take more than one of my clients by surprise. Yet I submit the following:

Convention	Agencies are structures lacking organization.
Disruption	Agencies are fluid spaces in which there is room for everyone to perform at his or her best.
Vision	Agencies' configurations prefigure tomorrow's organizations.

One of Disruption's benefits is that it enhances the horizontality of the agency. Disruption encourages people from various business clusters to work on a given problem together. To become fluid groups of problem solvers that don't look for answers next door. Everyone is enriched by the presence of others. In any company, and in any agency, the common goal is to drive people to bring out their best.

Advertisers and Advisers

Downstream tactics are steadily becoming inseparable from upstream strategy. The separation of the two is proving more and more artificial. A strategy derives its value only from its execution. The strategy's feasibility is itself a criterion for judging its validity.

Lou Gerstner recently said, "Implementation is strategy." According to Harrison McCain, "Opportunism is strategic." Ries and Trout, as we have noted, insist that tactics are strategies. Because agencies are tactic experts, they become legitimate when it comes to strategy consulting.

Ries and Trout cannot be said to be great fans of advertising agencies. Yet they sense the degree to which mastery of the downstream can inspire the upstream, by a kind of feedback effect. In *Bottom Up Marketing*, they assert that you have to start from the specific to get to the general. In other words, to "find a tactic that will work and then build it into a strategy." They take "Pizza Pizza," Federal Express, and Burger King as their examples. They even go on to say that tactics are often advertising ideas and offer an unexpected reversal of roles by claiming that "the advertising tactic should dictate business strategy."

I won't say this is not an exaggeration. But the thought is certainly provocative. They believe that tactics belong to the world of ideas, and not strategy. And these days what makes the difference is, of course, ideas. You must begin with the idea, then work backward and check it against the data.

Bottom, top. Downstream, upstream. Backward, forward. This vocabulary reflects the thinking. We must break with the rationality of top-down thinkers. Free ourselves from linear thinking. Trust our intuition. Reward an idea's originality more than a strategy's relevance.

So goes the old debate between idealism and empiricism. Between deduction and induction. We titled one of our more recent presentations to UAP, "Induction Marketing." While this term may sound a bit pretentious, it implies a very pertinent approach. Our "You're either number one or you're not" commercials for UAP reflect the company's self-imposed challenge of addressing and solving society's most critical problems, such as retirement and social security. It is the very message of these ads to the public at large that motivates each internal effort undertaken. In other words, it is the advertising campaign itself that pushes UAP to go further, to live up to the seemingly unattainable goal of constantly outdoing itself. In the five years that this campaign has been on the air, UAP's marketing department has been forced to come up with products and services worthy of its message. Today, UAP guarantees it will reply within 48 hours of a claim's submission. This "UAP Pact" would never have taken hold without our ads and, above all, without the company's "Penalty of Leadership" mind-set. Not long ago, UAP's managing director shared this with me.

What's so surprising about this? Are we guilty of stepping beyond our bounds? No. Advertising, whose role is to glorify everything marketing does, is in return justified in asking marketing to go the extra yard: to do just a bit more.

This dialectical move upstream from downstream is an illustration of the feedback effect which exists in all organic systems. The brain, for example, dictates muscular contractions that are sometimes too strong; this excess is signaled by nerve impulses to the brain—in other words, pain, which in turn alters its control mechanisms. This is a well-known example. The same rules apply to, among other things, cybernetics. Cybernetics conceives systems that are capable of both applying algorithms and using the result itself as a means of modifying the algorithm used. This retroaction is the cornerstone of artificial intelligence research. Advertising people are like muscles or artificial intelligence. They spend their time making round-trips from deduction to induction, from the upstream down and back up again.

Intuition in matters downstream produces a stronger strategy. Our ads about the Danone Institute encouraged our client to delve even deeper into the issue of health. Our Virgin posters reinforced the role that the company had claimed for itself. The same thing can be said for our UAP commercials and Oil of Olay campaigns. The cogency of the executions told us we had made the right strategic choices. Downstream validated upstream. Tactics reinforced strategies.

It is in this sense that agencies are useful strategic consultants. They live in a concrete, pragmatic world. The are in touch with and feel reality. Their thinking is agile and enables them to visualize worlds of possibilities better than any other outside consultant. There is no way you can envision the future of a brand without imagination—the future cannot be extrapolated. Our role is not to solve clients' problems, but to make new possibilities take shape. To come up with the ideas that generate a better share of the future for our clients, as follows:

Convention	Agencies should stick to crafting ads.
Disruption	Agencies are in the business of creating possibilities.
Vision	Our role is to imagine our clients' share of the future.

An agency's internal culture is a contributing factor in strengthening its competitive edge. It's the only place where marketing and creative people coexist. In other words, two opposing mind-sets. Simplistically speaking, they symbolize the deductive and the inductive. Yet these people work together all the time, and thus create a common culture among themselves. The combining, or rather the fusion, of these two worlds is an invaluable asset. An irreplaceable weapon.

Agencies have to realize this—that they are unique. All they have to do is exploit their horizontality to its fullest, to live and breathe the notion of working together. *Transversality*, the ability to get people of disparate backgrounds to think together every day, goes beyond mere pluridisciplinarity, which is simply about people from different fields working together. For me, transversality is all agencies' raison d'être, because it redistributes the scope of reflection and magnifies the powers of the imagination.

More than any consulting firm, an ad agency can think beyond boundaries. Focus on the "big picture." And imagine larger visions.

A Battle of Ideas

Global. Instantaneous. Dematerialized. It's clear that the economy is entering a new phase. It's not a mere evolution but a real revolution that's going to take place in the new millennium. Immaterial value will determine material value. French sociologist Leo Scher has written that the relationship between the sign and the object is being reversed. "The sign," he says, "is becoming more real than the object and the object more virtual than the sign." We have entered the "all-cultural" age.

The world of the concrete has less value and interest. It's added culture, the dose of knowledge injected into products, which gives them their value and confers meaning on them. This knowledge is often a savoir faire, a concrete human skill. But more and more, it's also immaterial know-how, a conception of an object's finality, a value system that determines its value of meaning. Whether it's perfume or yogurt, the value of meaning will prevail over material value. Immaterial value lasts longer.

People have long believed that the role of communication was to add a touch of color and desirability to a product. To highlight its specificity or make up for the lack thereof. This end-of-the-assembly-line mind-set is no longer valid. Communication is not a mere product attribute. It is an integral part of its makeup. It goes beyond bringing a product into contact with consumers. It becomes the palpable cultural value of the product.

Here's how this idea looks, outlined in our Disruption format:

Convention	The real world is a world of tangibles.
Disruption	Intangible assets are becoming durable.
Vision	Brand culture is the product's ultimate asset.

For 20 years, advertising people have sought to create a difference in economies of concrete goods. From now on, advertising will create added value in economies made up of more and more intangibles. The battle of brands and products will be, above all, a battle of ideas. Consuming a product will be tantamount to adhering to or, better yet, voting for a brand's culture.

Disruption is the motor for value creation. By defining the vision, it gives brands head starts. In its reference to conventions, it relegates competitors to the past. The great brands of this end of the century are those that have succeeded in conveying their vision by questioning certain conventions, whether it's Apple's humanist vision, which reverses the relationship between people and machines; Benetton's libertarian vision, which overthrows communication conventions; Microsoft's progressive vision, which topples bureaucratic barriers; or Virgin's anticonformist vision, which rebels against the powers that be.

In this ever-growing battle for ideas, we have made Disruption our internal culture, our business capability. Something anchored in our mentality, written into our genetic code.

It's a way of thinking, which is not to say a doctrine. It consists of a body of opinions and attitudes. As we've seen, it stimulates the creativity of the strategy. It resists the linearity that transforms the advertising process into an assembly line. It looks less for differences than for likenesses among brands and translates those similarities into conventions that may then be thrown into question. It's not afraid of leading to category advertising, because it seeks to make every brand a category in itself.

Disruption is our common culture. Its transversality overthrows hierarchies within the same offices and erases the boundaries separating offices in different countries. When an account executive from New York talks on the phone with his or her French counterpart about a convention in a given market, they can immediately delve deeper into the heart of the brand's problems. Discussions are fertile and enlightening. No more superficial exchanges that barely touch upon the problems and skirt the issues. Disruption puts people on the same wavelength; thoughts don't need to be spelled out. Half-words are enough. Disruption creates a context that promotes free exchange.

In the digital age, we are going to be overwhelmed with data. Many fear that we are entering an era of information overflow, but one devoid of ideas. We believe that the inverse will occur, that we're entering a world of ideas. The battle will be fierce. As the world becomes more complex, the balance between power and ideas will shift in favor of ideas. This is what I hope for, and what I believe is starting to happen. Even the most powerful companies cannot successfully block the diffusion of any creative idea, such as a revolutionary computer program. The venues to share information are infinite. Contemporary communication short-circuits power. Ideas will be the sole justification for authority.

Just think about the word *authority*. It is derived from *author*, an individual who creates ideas. Now that the table is turning, ideas will become the new source of power. The author will regain authority.

Straddled between two millennia, the next decade will herald in new ways of living and working, new value systems. Rupture will be inherent. Intelligence will reside in movement. And in the awareness that what remains to be discovered is more important than what has already been discovered. Today's visions will be tomorrow's conventions.

DISRUPTION WEB SITE

MANY OF THE campaigns cited in *Disruption* as well as an interactive version of the book can be found on the Disruption web site:

http://www.disruption.com

ACKNOWLEDGMENTS

DISRUPTION IS THE way of thinking of our whole company. It concerns all the people of BDDP, many of whom have contributed to perfecting and enriching this concept and, hence, the content of this book.

I would first of all like to thank Robin Lemberg, Nicole Cooper, Sarah Baldwin, and Hervé Brunette.

Robin's role was invaluable. She was my book doctor and jack-of-all-trades, with me from the very beginning of this project. She researched, analyzed, and interpreted pertinent material. She helped me reshape some of the text. With her American eye, she was instrumental in helping me to adapt the book for the American public. Without Robin, this book simply would not exist.

I would like to thank Nicole Cooper, my right hand for the last 15 years, who has spent as much time as myself on this book. Nicole's organization and patience kept everything going. I thank Nicole for her devotion and her talent.

This book was conceived and written in both French and English. It's to Sarah Baldwin that I owe the perfect translation: Thanks to her, the spirit of the English book remains very close to its French version.

Hervé Brunette is, among other things, "Mr. Disruption" and the person responsible for perfecting the Disruption World Bank and the What-If Process and creating the Disruption University. Each day for the last

ACKNOWLEDGMENTS

five years, he has meditated on Disruption. Hervé took a fragile concept and made it solid and durable.

I would also like to thank all the people who, in some way or another, contributed to this book: Frank Assumma, Douglas Atkin, Chris Baker, Nicolas Bordas, Fiona Clancy, Isabelle Domercq, Pascal Dupont, Patrick Flaherty, Michael Greenlees, Andrew Jaffe, Michael Mark, Natalie Rastoin, Michel Sara, Eric Tong Cuong, and Rod Wright. And also Djazia Boukhelif, Philippe Gadel, Philippe Jacquot, Alastair Maclean, Corinne Vacher, and Phyllis Wagner.

Finally, a special tribute to my partners Marie-Catherine Dupuy, Jean-Claude Boulet, Jean-Michel Carlo, and Jean-Pierre Petit, without whom BDDP would never have existed nor would many of the campaigns described in this book.

BIBLIOGRAPHY

Ansoff, H. Igor. *The New Corporate Strategy.* New York: John Wiley & Sons, 1988.

Bijon, Claude. *Les Stratégies de Rupture*. Paris: Seuil, 1991.

Clancy, Kevin J., and Robert S. Shulman. *The Marketing Revolution: A Radical Manifesto for Dominating the Marketplace*. New York: HarperCollins, 1991.

D'Aveni, Richard A. *Hypercompetition*. New York: Free Press, 1994.

De Bono, Edward. *Serious Creativity*. New York: HarperCollins, 1992.

Dru, Jean-Marie. *Le Saut Créatif*. France: JCLattès, 1984.

Gale, Bradley T. *Managing Customer Value*. New York: Free Press, 1994.

Hamel, Gary, and C. K. Prahalad. *Competing for the Future*. Boston: Harvard Business School Press, 1994.

Hammer, Michael, and James Champy. *Reengineering the Corporation*. New York: HarperCollins, 1993.

Handy, Charles. *The Age of Unreason*. Boston: Harvard Business School Press, 1990.

Handy, Charles. *The Empty Raincoat*. London: Hutchinson, 1994.

Heller, Robert. *The Super Chiefs*. New York: Truman Talley Books, 1992.

Jagdish and Parikh. *Intuition: The New Frontier of Management*. Oxford, U.K.: Blackwell Publishers, 1995.

Kapferer, Jean-Noël. *Strategic Brand Management*. New York: Free Press, 1992.

Kriegel, Robert J., and Louis Patler. *If It Ain't Broke . . . Break It!* New York: Warner Books, 1991.

Lele, Milind M. *Creating Strategic Leverage: Matching Company Strengths with Market Opportunities.* New York: John Wiley & Sons, 1992.

Magrath, Allan J. *The Six Imperatives of Marketing.* New York: AMACOM, 1992.

Martin, Justin. "Ignore Your Customer." *Fortune* (May 1995).

Mayer, Martin. *Whatever Happened to Madison Avenue.* Boston: Little, Brown, 1991.

Mitroff, Ian I., and Harold A. Linstone. *The Unbounded Mind.* New York: Oxford University Press, 1993.

Naisbitt, John. *Global Paradox: The Bigger the World's Economy, the More Powerful Its Smaller Players.* London: Nicholas Brealey Publishing, 1994.

Ohmae, Kenichi. *The Mind of a Strategist: The Art of Japanese Business.* New York: McGraw-Hill, 1982.

Peters, Tom. *The Pursuit of WOW: Every Person's Guide to Topsy-Turvy Times.* London: Pan Books, 1993.

Peters, Tom. *Thriving on Chaos: Handbook for a Management Revolution.* New York: Harper & Row, 1987.

Peters, Tom. *The Tom Peter's Seminar.* London: Pan Books, 1994.

Porges, K. Shelly. Bank of America, Senior Vice President. Interview (September, 1989).

Rapp, Stan, and Tom Collins. *MaxiMarketing: The New Direction in Advertising, Promotion, & Marketing Strategy.* New York: McGraw-Hill, 1987.

Ray, Michael, and Rochelle Myers. *Creativity in Business.* New York: Doubleday, 1986.

Ries, Al, and Jack Trout. *Bottom-Up Marketing.* New York: Plume, 1990.

Ries, Al, and Jack Trout. *Marketing Warfare.* New York: Plume, 1986.

Ries, Al, and Jack Trout. *Positioning: The Battle for Your Mind.* New York: Warner Books, 1986.

Thomas, Robert J. *New Product Success Stories.* New York: John Wiley & Sons, 1995.

Toffler, Alvin. *La Troisième Vague* (The Third Wave). Paris: Denoël, Gonthier, 1980.

Toffler, Alvin. *Les Nouveaux Pouvoirs* (Powershift). Paris: Fayard, 1992.

Treacy, Michael, and Fred Wiersema. *The Discipline of Market Leaders*. Reading, Mass.: Addison-Wesley, 1995.

Waterman, Robert H., Jr. *What America Does Right*. New York: Plume, 1995.

ADVERTISING CAMPAIGNS

Agency*	Campaign
Abbott Mead Vickers	Sainsbury
Ally & Gargano	Federal Express
Ammirati & Puris/Lintas	Johnson & Johnson Baby Powder
BBDO	Kookai (CLM), Leclerc (CLM), Macintosh Powerbook, Pepsi, Phildar (CLM), Polaroid, Total (CLM)
BDDP	Amora, BMW, Caisses D'Epargne, Caprice des Dieux, Danone, France Telecom, Hachette, Hertz, Keds, Kronenbourg, McCain, McDonald's, Michelin, Playskool, Porto Cruz, Printemps, Public Water Works, Rodier, SNCF, Sogo Fashion Stores, TAG Heuer, 3 Suisses, Toys "Я" Us, UAP, UPSA, Virgin
BDDP (BST)	BBC, Classic FM, Oddbins, Scrumpy Jack

* Campaigns cited, not necessarily current agency.

Agency	Campaign
BDDP (Wells Rich Greene)	Clairol Herbal Essences, Dun & Bradstreet, Ford Motor Company, Health-o-Meter, Hertz, Liberty Mutual, Oil of Olay, Pringles, TAG Heuer, Toys "Я" Us
BBH	Levi's, Murphy's Irish Stout, Phileas Fogg, Toohey's Export Beer
BMP	John Smith's Bitters
Barro/Testa	Zanussi
Bates	Avis, Heinz
Batey Ads	Singapore Airlines
Chiat/Day	Apple, Eveready Energizer, Infiniti, Nike, Reebok
Cliff Freeman & Partners	Little Caesars
Collet Dickenson Pearce	Benson & Hedges
Cossette	Molson Grand Nord, TVE
Creative Artists Agency	Coca-Cola
DDB Needham	Budweiser, New York Lottery, Nana, Volkswagen
DMB&B	Charmin, Galaxy, Vicks
Deutsch Inc.	IKEA
Dupuy Compton	Ariel, Monsavon
Eccla	Cassino
Euro RSCG	Crédit Agricole, Darty, Evian, Head & Shoulders, MCI (MVBMS), NASDAQ (MVBMS)

Agency	Campaign
Fallon McElligott	Lee Jeans, National Basketball Association, *Rolling Stone*, *The Wall Street Journal*
FCA	Woolmark
Foote, Cone & Belding	Coors Lite, Levi's for Women, Dockers
Goodby, Berlin & Silverstein	California Milk Processor Board, Chevy's Mexican Restaurants, The Good Guys!, Norwegian Cruise Lines
Hal Riney & Partners	Bartles & Jaymes, Saturn
Howell Henry Chaldecott Lury	Tango
In House	Benetton, MTV, Seibu
Kirshenbaum & Bond	Citibank, Keds, Snapple
J. Walter Thompson	Listerine
Lawler Ballard Advertising	First National Bank of Commerce
Leap Partnership	Miller Lite
Leo Burnett Co.	Cheer, Gleem, Hallmark, Kellogg's Corn Flakes, Marlboro, McDonald's, 7-Up
Lintas	*The Economist*
Lowe Howard & Spink	Heineken UK, Tesco
Lowe & Partners/SMS	Diet Coke, Sprite
McCann-Erickson	Solo (JBR Reklamebrya), Taster's Choice
McManus	Cadillac 1921
North Castle Partners Adv. Inc.	Ocean Spray

ADVERTISING CAMPAIGNS

Agency	Campaign
N. W. Ayer & Partners	AT&T
Ogilvy & Mather	Duracell, Guinness, IBM, Maxwell House, Sominex
Publicis	Nescafé
Saatchi & Saatchi	British Airways, British Telecom, Castelmaine XXXX, Dunlop, Silk Cut
TBWA	Absolut Vodka, Club Med USA
Taxi Jaune	Maison Phénix
Team One	Lexus
Warwick Baker & Fiore	Murphy's Irish Stout
Wieden & Kennedy	Microsoft, Nike, OK Cola
Young & Rubicam	Crest, Dentyne, Flash, Jell-O, Orangina, Smirnoff, Union Bank of Switzerland (Adrico)

INDEX

ABOUT THE AUTHOR

JEAN-MARIE DRU is a founder and the chairman of the BDDP Group, a leading worldwide communications company. Founded in 1984, BDDP is the youngest and fastest-growing group among the top 15 international communications networks. In 1991, the BDDP Group acquired Wells Rich Greene, a prominent U.S. agency. Today, BDDP is present in 27 countries, employs 2,200 people, and enjoys $1.5 billion in annual billings.

A graduate of HEC business school, Mr. Dru began his advertising career with Dupuy Compton (now Saatchi & Saatchi) as an account executive on Procter & Gamble and went on to become executive creative director. In 1977, Mr. Dru joined Young & Rubicam in Paris as managing director and became CEO in 1979.

Mr. Dru is the author of a book published in 1985 on creative ideas in advertising, entitled *Le Saut Créatif*. His more recent work has been published in leading French business magazines and periodicals. Mr. Dru is also a frequent speaker on "Disruption," a methodology for creating powerful business and advertising strategies.

Currently vice president of the French National Advertising Association and a member of the European Advertising Association, Mr. Dru also served as president of the Cannes Advertising Film Festival Jury in 1983 and president of the Outdoor Advertising Grand Prix in 1987 and 1988.

Mr. Dru resides in Paris with his wife and five children.